"Having a big idea is one thing, but relentlessly pursuing it and prioritising actions around it is what will ensure success. This book gives you some really good tools, and then holds your hand to make sure you take action. I really enjoyed it."

Guy Levine, CEO & Founder, Return On Digital

"Simply brilliant. An immensely practical and valuable tool for anyone in business."

Steve Pipe, Author of _How to Build a Better Business and Make More Money_

"Distilled wisdom and the space for you to use it and develop it for your own life and business. Well researched, organised and beautifully laid out. Use it and make this your best year yet."

Tim Johnson, Managing Director, www.meaningfulsuccess.co.uk

"If you struggle to implement all that you would like to in your business, and would like a mentor in a book to tell you what to do, how to do it and to make sure that you do it, then you will be delighted that you bought this book."

Nick Jervis, Law Firm Growth Expert, www.samsonconsulting.co.uk

"The _Check-in Strategy Journal_ gives me — and my CEO clients — an otherwise priceless opportunity: A daily, virtual meeting with Robert and Adam, setting immediate intention toward strategically sound action."

Artie Isaac, CEO Peer Group Leader, Columbus, Ohio

"Adam and Robert bring creativity, common sense and process to achieving goals in this _Check In Strategy Journal_. Let's go!"

Julie Nimmons, CEO/EXO Living, Vistage Chair

CHECK·IN STRATEGY JOURNAL

YOUR DAILY TRACKER FOR BUSINESS AND PERSONAL DEVELOPMENT

ROBERT CRAVEN · ADAM HARRIS

WILEY

This edition first published 2017
© 2017 Robert Craven and Adam Harris

Registered office
John Wiley & Sons Ltd, The Atrium, Southern Gate, Chichester, West Sussex, PO19 8SQ, United Kingdom

For details of our global editorial offices, for customer services and for information about how to apply for permission to reuse the copyright material in this book please see our website at www.wiley.com.

Library of Congress Cataloging-in-Publication Data is available

A catalogue record for this book is available from the British Library.

ISBN 978-1-119-31807-1 (pbk)

10 9 8 7 6 5 4 3 2 1

Cover design/image: Jody Stenning

Set in 8/11 Roboto by Aptara

Printed in Great Britain by TJ International Ltd, Padstow, Cornwall, UK

For Cal, Jessie, Bonnie and Ben. And Thea.

Robert

For... my wife Naomi, with whom I have shared so much already and more to come, especially with Amelie our eldest and Evelin our youngest.

My Dad, Steve, not only my father but also a great friend who has pulled me back when needed.

My Mum, Bev, and brother, Lee, whilst not always knowing what I was doing always encouraged me.

My Grandma Rose, her repetitive stories always had meaning and wise words.

My Grandma Fran, who sadly never saw what I have become, but always believed that I would.

Robert French, a guide, supporter and believer, who saw what I couldn't, and helped me lay the first bricks of what I do now.

My Vistage Studio VI cohort who helped me "grow up".

Artie Isaac, my challenger, friend and coach.

Adam

CONTENTS

ACKNOWLEDGEMENTS

We'd like to thank everyone who has helped and worked with us to create the *Check-In Strategy Journal*.

Special thanks go to our clients, associates, friends and of course, our families. Without them none of this would have been possible. They have contributed to and road-tested the Journal and shown to us that it significantly improves people's lives and their businesses. We are humbled by the results we have witnessed.

Finally, big thanks go to Team DC, especially Jaime and Tricia.

Robert and Adam

INTRODUCTION

Running a business is not easy. It is certainly not as easy as the books make out... or is it?

In our roles as directors and consultants to numerous businesses, we have learnt that the key ingredients of success include the following:

1. Agree where you are now
2. Agree where you are going
3. Agree how you are going to get there
4. Take massive action
5. Be accountable for the execution and the results.

And this Journal helps you to do all five things. It is as simple as that.

We just don't get our feet held to the fire enough!

Recently, a colleague stated the obvious,

> " Even if there is a plan, most business directors just don't get their feet held to the fire to deliver on promises and commitments. We find ways to wriggle out of delivering. And we, and the business, suffer as a result. "

The logical reply is that a coach or a mastermind group may be the answer. However, there is another option, which would be a "device" or "mechanism" that enables the director to take ownership of the accountability and the reflection for themselves. Hence, the birth of this Check-in Journal.

The Journal is a place to check-in. You check-in to preview, review, update or modify your activities, plans and goals. The process of checking-in is about setting time aside to get your thoughts, ideas and processes in order.

Robert and Adam

The Robert/Adam partnership is a partnership of skills. Robert is often described as Mr "Strategy". On the other hand, Adam is known as Mr "People and Culture". A fantastic combination, because you simply can't do one without the other. Strategy + Culture = Success.

Robert is likely to say,

 Without strategy, execution is aimless. Without execution, strategy is useless. 🙶

—Morris Chang

Adam, on the other hand, will quote,

 Culture eats strategy for breakfast. 🙶

—Peter Drucker

Too right: culture underpins everything.

What this Journal does is get you to define your strategy, your plans, your goals and what you need to make it all happen.

Who is the Journal for?

The Journal has been focused on key decision-makers in business. Anyone running a board, a business, a business unit or a department. Anyone who needs to create clarity and focus about what they are trying to achieve. Busy people with lots to do who need to prioritise as well as monitor and evaluate their performance and achievements.

For not-for-profit as well as for-profit use?

This Journal and the planning tools have been used with charities, not-for-profits, housing associations and even the British Council.

What's the split in the focus between business and personal development?

Great question. Our experience is that most decision-makers need to balance their business and their personal ambitions, drive and focus. High divorce rates associated with highly ambitious execs are because of their failure to recognise the need to balance the two worlds. We work to live and not the other way around!

In terms of page count, there appears to be more emphasis on business development. However, in terms of impact on your thinking and planning, it is usually the few personal development pages, with their straightforward, no-nonsense questions, that get people thinking and reflecting. Please do *not* skip over them! Any one question might get you thinking really carefully and it can take you anything from minutes to hours to days to answer the question properly. (And asking the same question 12 months later might well evoke an entirely different response!)

Why use the Journal?

The Journal lets you map out your strategy and plans in real time, on paper, and map out your annual, quarterly, monthly, weekly and daily goals and targets. More importantly, it enables you to measure and monitor your results and offers feedback, ideas and pointers to help you improve your performance. This is quite a personal and reflective exercise.

Our experience is that the Journal becomes a fundamental part of your planning and setting up of each week, month and quarter. Essentially, it helps you to take control of your schedule: both your business and personal life will benefit!

Two quotes spring to mind here,

 What gets measured gets done. ”

—Attributed to Tom Peters

 If you can measure it you can manage it. ”

—Rheticus

What the Journal is not

A simple diary. A checklist. A clever clogs theory. A touchy-feely plaything. A nice Christmas gift to be ignored. Just another business book. A navel-gazing exercise. Pompous.

Our "ology"

The thinking behind the Journal is as follows:

1. *"Keep it simple but powerful"* – Like a triple espresso. Right for people who want to get to the point quickly (but give them access to further support if they want it)
2. *"Be practical and results-focused"*
3. *"Share stuff that works"* – Use what works in other businesses
4. *"Start with the end in mind"* [Stephen Covey]
5. *"If you always do what you've always done you will always get what you've always got"* [Attributed to Anthony Robbins, Albert Einstein, Henry Ford, Mark Twain...]
6. *"Change is uncomfortable but the results can be life changing... for the better"*
7. *"Everything should be made as simple as possible but not simpler"* [Albert Einstein]
8. *"We're all responsible for whatever life we have!"*

The structure of this book

Part One is the triple espresso set of tools to complete ahead of using Part Two, which is the Journal.

Part One:

Part One contains a series of discrete yet interlocking tools. Completing them will enable you to get the maximum benefit from Part Two, the Journal. The more preparation and reflection you do ahead of starting the Journal, the more benefit you will get from using the Journal day by day, week by week, year by year.

Part One starts with:

- **Wheel of Life**

  to look at the big picture of business and personal goals.

In the *Business Planning* section, we work on:

- **Performance to date**

  to understand where the business is now

- **Three-year goals**

  to understand where we want to be

- **Cascade map**

  from purpose through vision to mission to strategy to milestones and KPIs, to map out from the big picture through to the detail

- **Wallpaper exercise**

  to map out the steps on the way

- **Annual Business Plan**

  to articulate key business initiatives and goals.

In the *Personal Planning* section, we work on:

- **Probably Your Best Year Yet exercise**

  to assess and evaluate your key roles and priorities

- **Annual Personal Plan**

  to articulate key business initiatives and goals.

The Check-in journey

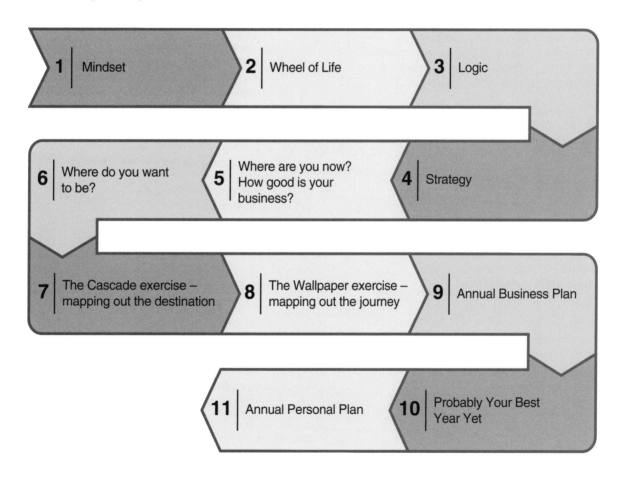

1 | Mindset
2 | Wheel of Life
3 | Logic
4 | Strategy
5 | Where are you now? How good is your business?
6 | Where do you want to be?
7 | The Cascade exercise – mapping out the destination
8 | The Wallpaper exercise – mapping out the journey
9 | Annual Business Plan
10 | Probably Your Best Year Yet
11 | Annual Personal Plan

Part Two

Armed with your completed *Annual Business Plan* and your *Annual Personal Plan*, you can proceed to start working on Part Two: The Journal. The Journal section is full of tools, tips and techniques to help you become more effective at delivering on your goals, day by day, week by week, month by month, quarter by quarter.

Part Three

Part Three is a series of additional exercises that supplement those found in Part One.

Although Part One acts as a standalone series of exercises, Part Three acts as instant access to additional exercises that support and underpin the Part One exercises. They are not felt to be 100% essential, but they will significantly add to the value you get out of the Journal. These are the tip of the iceberg of additional resources, tools and exercises – as well as videos and case studies – that can be found at the website **www.checkinjournal.com/thehub.**

But where to start the Journal and how to use it?

Great question.

The hardest thing is to get started... So, what's stopping you from starting now? Some people say "but it looks so nice" or "I don't know what to do first". The solution is to write your name in the front and simply begin using the Journal. Just start by taking action!

Some (most) people literally start at the beginning and work their way through the book, a page at a time. They work through the Planning section over, say, a weekend, then they work through the Journal itself day by day, week by week.

Others skip the planning and go straight for the Journal.

Some get so much value from the planning that they actually put the Journal down and share their new-found "aha" knowledge with the team. Then maybe they return to the Journal section at a later stage.

Others dip in and dip out as the mood takes them. This is not recommended, but the point is this: this is *your* Journal for *you* and for *your* business. You use it how you feel you can use it best. We do not want to be zealously over-prescriptive and suggest that there is one way and only one way to apply the ology.

Planning: What comes first, business or personal development?

We see *business* and *personal development* as equally important. We'd love to say that one is significantly more important than the other, but that simply is not the case. They are interlocking, interconnecting pieces of a jigsaw. It is no good just focusing on one and ignoring the other. In effect, start where you feel most comfortable.

What part of the Journal gives the biggest bang for the buck?

The answer to this question really depends on what kind of organisation you work for and how much time you have spent reflecting on your own personal goals and ambitions.

Executives of larger organisations with a prescriptive planning process love the simplicity of our process and how it enables them to boil business planning down to the essentials. The personal planning reminds them of why they are doing it all in the first place!

Owners of smaller businesses love the structure and framework that they can apply to their business and private lives.

Planning: How long?

We suggest at least a couple of hours. It is all self-explanatory but there is further help (videos, articles and worksheets), if needed, at www.checkinjournal.com/thehub.

If you are in a business that regularly undergoes business planning, then you may find it relatively easy to transfer your experience into our template. If you are less familiar with business planning, you may have to work quite hard to create the business fundamentals from first principles for yourself. Likewise, you may find the personal development piece either easy – because you are familiar with this type of thinking and questioning – or quite difficult – maybe even awkward if it's new to you. But don't worry; it will all make sense rapidly.

Once completed, you can transfer the relevant pieces to the Journal, and start off on Week 1.

Just another time-management tool to discard like most New Year resolutions?

The last thing we need is another time-management app. What we all need is something that will enable us to decide what we are going to do, help us to plan and do it and help us track our performance and learn from it. That's what the Journal does. And it becomes addictive! Why? Because you feel you are taking control and you can see the benefits first-hand. You have been warned!

What happens if I have the Journal but it's not the New Year?

It's easy to flick through the Journal and put it back on the shelf. Or you might say to yourself, "I will start it when…". Our recommendation is just start, no matter the month! Procrastination is not going to help you or your future.

Next steps

 Take action, take massive action! There is no time like the present. Hope is not a method. **,,**

—Robert and Adam

PART 1

PLANNING

The *Planning* section is a concentrated version of what you need to do to create and write down your plans and goals for the coming year. It is divided into two parts: *Business Planning* and *Personal Planning*.

The format we are introducing has been used with literally thousands of businesses since Robert's days at Warwick Business School. We use it because it works. It is simple. It focuses on key issues. It is in plain language and free of jargon. People who use it grasp the idea very quickly, apply it to their business and see buy-in and results.

This material has been used with everyone from peer-to-peer groups to boards of directors. It has been the centre-piece of everything from five-day board retreats to 40-minute immersives.

The following pages cover the key elements used with business directors to define and clarify their business and personal futures. We have gone straight to the heart of the matter and avoided using anything we do not feel is absolutely necessary.

Please note, it looks deceptively simple!

The power is in the process of actually working through the worksheets. The power is in simplifying things and focusing on what really matters. This can be done in an hour or so or can become part of a company-wide, full-blown business planning exercise. The choice is yours. Choose what works for you.

How most people use the Journal

Most people choose to run through the *planning* worksheets on their own. The worksheets give a different slant on how they may already be doing business planning in their own business. Because of its focus on simplifying and focusing, it helps to clarify more complex planning systems. It highlights key tasks for the individual.

I got the most value out of the planner section by going through it on my own. A quiet room, a large jug of coffee or two, a calculator and lots of post-its. It helped me crystallise exactly what I was trying to achieve and what steps I needed to take. **"**

—Jamie Collins, CEO

" The planning section really helped me to clarify exactly what I was trying to do both in the business and, funnily enough, in my private life. We now use the business planning tools throughout the business. To be honest, we had been playing at planning before. The Journal brings simplicity and focus to the business. As a consequence we feel more in control and we are hitting our targets like never before! "

—Jodie Patterson, Managing Director

" Having looked at some of the exercises, we realised that the board would get even more benefit if we pulled in an external facilitator to walk us through the exercise. That way we could concentrate on the thinking as someone else ran the session. "

—Jessica Nelson, CEO

Using the Journal

Wherever you see an exercise in the Journal, please be aware that the instructions are only a guide to how the tool can be used. Some of these exercises can be rolled out over an entire day so you can dig deeper and probe to get more understanding. The self-same exercises can often be completed in a matter of 10 minutes. Clearly the impact varies with the effort you put in and how engaged you are in the process.

To be clear, we recommend that most of the exercises be completed in 10–20 minutes. We are all busy and often we "get" the message or we "get" the point quite quickly. If, however, you come across an exercise that you want to explore further, then feel free to do so.

We, as authors, don't like overly prescriptive processes that squeeze the creativity out of an exercise; we imagine that you feel the same. Included in the *planning* part of the Journal are our preferred versions of models. That is because we do not believe that there is ONE universal perfect model and think that different versions have different purposes.

What most readers do is run through most of the exercises in an afternoon. Yes, this may seem a little superficial, but it gives people a sense of the whole and a sense of the individual parts. Then, at their own leisure, people return to the exercises that they feel they should work on some more.

If you have a coach or a buddy, challenging and being challenged allows you to think of things that you wouldn't normally think of. These exercises work in a similar fashion.

The website www.checkinjournal.com has video instructions for each exercise.

What we'll cover:

- Mindset
- Wheel of Life
- Logic
- Strategy
- Where are you now? How good is your business?
- Where do you want to be?
- The Cascade exercise – mapping out the destination
- The Wallpaper exercise – mapping out the journey
- Annual Business Plan
- Probably Your Best Year Yet
- Annual Personal Plan.

To find out more about how other businesses use the Check-in planning tools, visit www.checkinjournal.com/thehub.

Mindset: The one thing that determines everything else

No amount of the right tools, systems, processes and strategies will work if you or your team have the wrong mindset.

Too many business owners and directors do not have the right mindset. They spend too much time meddling, working *in* the business rather than working *on* the business. They get preoccupied with petty debates with staff or clients. Often we just don't think big enough.

Running through this Journal is the notion that we need to get our mindset in order. And fast.

The Check-In Journal links the planning and the execution.

 If I had eight hours to chop down a tree, I'd spend six hours sharpening my axe. **"**

—Abraham Lincoln

Next, we will start the planning exercises with the Wheel of Life exercise. It may sound a little touchy-feely but it is a great starting point that combines both business and personal aspects of your life.

Wheel of Life exercise: The big picture for business and personal growth

The first exercise, the Wheel of Life, is a big picture check-in to evaluate both your business and personal success. It is the start of our Part One exercises.

Why use the Wheel of Life?

This version is particularly powerful at getting you to address just how well you are performing in key aspects of your life. It identifies weaknesses and where you need to focus your energies.

What is it?

This is a *"where am I now?"* type exercise that you may have seen before. It looks at how well you are performing in such areas as family, career and fun. It is a snapshot *"how do I score myself right now?"* tool.

How to use it?

We recommend a minimum of 20 minutes to score yourself (see below).

Next, reflect on your scores on your own – or you may prefer to share and discuss the scores with your partner. This can take a long time (hours rather than minutes) but is worth the time investment.

Wheel of Life instructions

For each axis on the chart, mark a score between 0 and 10, where 0 is a low score and 10 is a high score.

Score where you are today and join the marks to create a kind of a circular shape.

People often ask, "What is a 7?" It's subjective and for you to score. Some people never score a 10 as it's "perfect". Whatever your scale is, it is your scale and the important thing to consider is what would +1 (one more) look like and why? And what would −1 (one less) look like and why?

The ability to stop, stand still and reflect is important. You need to understand where you have come from and where you are in order to understand where you want to go.

Other possible questions

- "Is it 7 and improving, 7 and getting worse, or just stuck at 7?"
- "Why haven't you given yourself 8 or 6?"
- "What would you need to do to improve the score?"
- "How can you justify your scores? Where is the evidence?"
- "Are you really sure that you are measuring appropriately?"

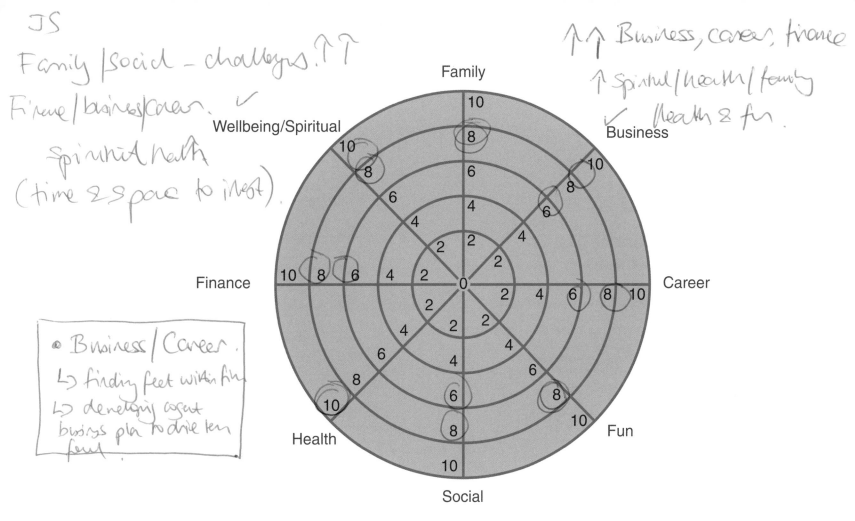

JS
Family / social – challenges. ↑↑
Finance / business / career. ✓
   Spiritual health
(time & space to invest).

↑↑ Business, career, finance
↑ Spiritual / health / family
✓ Health & fun.

• Business / Career.
↳ finding feet within firm
↳ developing cogent
business plan to drive term
fwd.

How do you score your Wheel of Life?

When asked to score yourself, it is worth asking:

- "How would I score myself on this aspect?"
- "What's worked/working?"
- "What's not worked/working?"

Where would you like to be?

Next, score where you would like the different aspects to be in, say, 12 months' time. Do this in a different colour.

Now, the questions to reflect on are:

- "How do I get from where I am now to where I want to be?"
- "What do I need to do more of, less of, stop doing, start doing and keep doing?"

15

Business Planning

A sense of logic: Working through the plan in a specific order

We spend too much time working *in* the business, dealing with the detail of keeping the business going. We do not spend enough time *on* the business: designing, planning and mapping out the future.

And when we do try to start working *on* the business, we usually start in the wrong place, simply reacting to the latest crisis – be it people, customers, growth or cash.

Working from the big picture down

Stepping back from the business makes us realise that we can be busy fools, madly chasing our tails but not sure if we are being busy at what is really important. Not sure if we even know what is really important. How do we find out?

There is a logical hierarchy for planning a business, to regain a sense of sanity in the proceedings.

There is an attractive simplicity in starting at the top with the big picture and creating the detail in the following order:

1) Strategy: Business strategy and planning
   - "Where are we going?"
2) Marketing: Winning business – sales and marketing
   - "How will we sell this stuff?"
3) Operations: Managing operations
   - "How will we make this happen?"
4) People and culture: Teams and relationships
   - "How will we work together to make this happen?"

A big BUT...

The *people and culture* piece is NOT fourth in importance; it is the fundamental foundation that underpins and runs through every other aspect of the business. It is the DNA!

Time for some definitions

Strategy
"planning while being aware of the outside environment"

Marketing
"why and how... we get which people... to buy what from us..."

Operations
"doing the doing": systems, and processes to deliver our product/service

People and Culture
"the backbone of the business".

Strategy: The first building block of the plan

Strategy at its simplest is asking: "Where are you going (while being aware of the outside environment)?"

The case for putting strategy at the head of the planning hierarchy is simple. In the real world,

 If you don't know where you're going then any road will do. ”

—Cheshire Cat, *Alice's Adventures in Wonderland*

Often, people attend badly run "Strategy Away-days" which create plans they rarely deliver on. The plans have little to do with the day to day running of their business. But it doesn't have to be that way.

The Cascade: A strategy/planning exercise that works

The Cascade is a simple yet powerful way to set up your business for the coming year(s). It comprises three apparently simple questions:

- "Where are you now?"
- "Where are you going?"
- "How are you going to get there?"

An additional question would be:

- "How are you going to measure and monitor your performance to make sure you stay on track (or take the necessary evasive action)?"

It creates the context for what you are doing this quarter, this month, this week... today.

The question the team asks

So, how do you answer the question that every member of your team is bound to ask at some point:

"What is our strategy?"

The essence, the heart, of the strategy needs to be articulated in a short, succinct statement. One that everyone can understand.

So, what is your business's strategy?

For us, a strategy is composed of three elements:

Objective

A single precise statement that will drive the business over the next three years.

Scope

The customer or service offering, location and position in the market.

Advantage

Sustainable competitive advantage (in other words, *"being different from or better than the rest and being able to maintain that position"*) is the essence of strategy. It comprises:

- your customer value proposition
- your unique activities.

You do need to write this down, but we are going to ask you to hang fire because the first piece in the strategy and planning jigsaw is to agree *"Where are you now?"* and *"How good is your business?"*

The Business Audit: Evaluating current performance

Having considered the big picture of the Wheel of Life, this exercise asks you to evaluate your current business performance. It's the start of looking at your business with the goal of being able to create a meaningful business plan you can monitor in your Journal.

Why use the "Where are you now?" Business Audit framework?

This apparently simple tool (also known as FiMO-PC) gives a clear indication of how good your business is and what needs to be worked on. It is a great springboard for lively conversation and debate (for instance, *"are we a 6 or a 7 and why?"*). It is a starting point for all future conversations about business performance when you ask, *"What are the scores on the doors?"*

What is it?

FiMO-PC is a *"where am I now?"* type exercise. It looks at how well your business is performing in finance, marketing, operations and people and culture. It is a snapshot *"how do I score myself right now?"* tool.

How to use it?

We recommend a minimum of 20 minutes to score yourself (see below).

Next, reflect on your scores – or you may prefer to share and discuss the scores with your business partner or your business team.

Tips

Keep asking the crunch questions:

- "What's worked/working?"
- "What's not worked/working?"
- "How do I get from where I am now to where I want to be?"
- "What do I need to do more of, less of, stop doing, start doing and keep doing?"

 The FiMO-PC exercise brought home to us exactly what we needed to do. In reality, we (as a team) already knew, but only when it was presented with such simplicity and clarity did the penny drop about the blindingly obvious of what we needed to do to sort out the business. And just in time!

—Andrea Higgins, Marketing Director

In order to answer the question, "*How good is your business?*", we use a framework referred to by the acronym FiMO-PC – Finance, Marketing and Operations underpinned by People and Culture.

FiMO-PC is a framework that can be used to evaluate the strengths and weaknesses of your business and to open up discussion to agree the "state of play".

Before you can look at future plans – your route map – you need to know how the business is performing right now.

Measuring business performance to date

When asked, "*What measures should be used to assess your company's performance to date?*" the same list of financials is usually put forward, give or take one or two differences (turnover, profit, cash, growth, etc.).

While these financial measures are commendable, to some degree they miss the point. What really matters is far more than just the financials.

While we don't dispute the importance of finance – it is poor financial performance that will make you go bust – you need to recognise that:

 Finance is simply a consequence of two other factors, marketing and operations... (and making those ingredients work depends on your people and culture working properly!) **"**

—Robert

So what?

To sort your *financial* performance, you probably need to sort your *marketing* and/or *operations* performance.

What do we mean by *marketing* and *operations?*

Marketing is all about finding prospects and selling to them. There are as many measures of *marketing* as there are measures of *finance*.

Operations is all about producing the service or product. It is all about the "doing". There are as many measures of *operations* as there are of *finance*.

Please note

The list under each box is just an indication of the sort of generic measures that a typical business might use.

So, how good is your business?

How would we measure your business performance to date? What measures would we use to evaluate how good your business is?

FiMO-PC exercise: Measuring performance to date

Score your business, now. Take 20–30 minutes.

Take each of the four main headings in the table below and give your business a score out of 10 for your performance (where 0 is a very low score and 10 is a very high score).

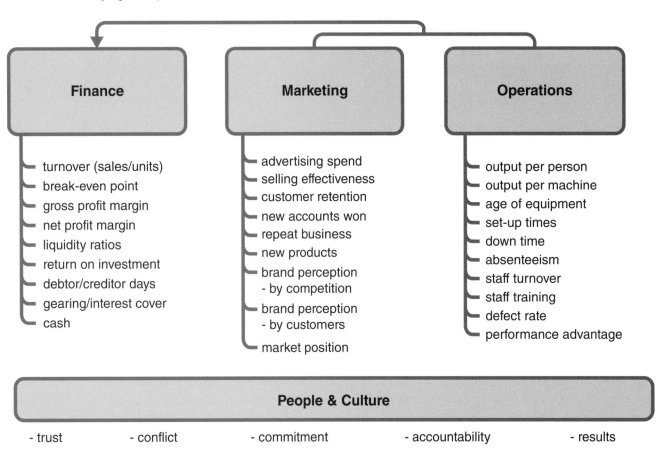

Finance

- turnover (sales/units)
- break-even point
- gross profit margin
- net profit margin
- liquidity ratios
- return on investment
- debtor/creditor days
- gearing/interest cover
- cash

Marketing

- advertising spend
- selling effectiveness
- customer retention
- new accounts won
- repeat business
- new products
- brand perception
  - by competition
- brand perception
  - by customers
- market position

Operations

- output per person
- output per machine
- age of equipment
- set-up times
- down time
- absenteeism
- staff turnover
- staff training
- defect rate
- performance advantage

People & Culture

- trust   - conflict   - commitment   - accountability   - results

How do the scores work?

Scores of *2* or *3* suggest that there is something seriously wrong

Scores of *4* or *5* or *6* suggest mediocrity

Scores of *8* or *9* suggest that you are pretty good if not heading towards "world class".

For more detail on FiMO-PC scoring, go to **www.checkinjournal.com/thehub**.

Action

So, here goes... mark your scores out of 10. Remember that this scoring system is subjective; it should be your gut response. By definition, this process is a little ambiguous and that is because we are interested in the process, the discussion about what the scores mean and how they can be improved. As soon as you enter a number, you (or your colleagues) can argue why the score given was either too high or too low.

Learning point

When scoring their own business, most people score something like this

Finance: 6

Marketing: 4

Operations: 8

People and Culture: 6

– i.e., *financial* performance is OK, *marketing* is pretty poor and we feel that we are pretty good at the *operations*, the doing. Meanwhile, *people and culture* is simply alright.

Please note:

- *Finance* is normally an average of *marketing* and *operations*.
- *People and culture* is *both* a consequence of, and cause of, *marketing* and *operations* performance! More on that later!

Key point

Recognise that we have four interlocking and overlapping functions, co-existing and interdependent. The image to be held in mind is that of a juggler – when all the balls move smoothly there are no problems, but if one ball starts to wobble then chaos often ensues.

Three morals here

First, to establish your journey, and direction, you need to know your "performance to date" (*"where are we now?"*).

Second, in order to improve your *financial* performance, it appears that you must first sort your *marketing* performance. However, we would actually say that first you need to check that your financial model is effective. There is no point growing sales if you are only making 1p in the £; first, sort your financial model so you make 10p in the £, then you should increase sales and marketing activity.

Third, none of the above mean anything if your *people and culture* piece is not working properly.

The Three-by-Three Strategy Matrix exercise: Three-year goals

While the previous exercise creates the starting point, "*where are you now?*", this next exercise looks at where you want to go. You will incorporate much of the thinking from this activity into later exercises, as well as use it as a beacon or a guide in your day-by-day, week-by-week use of the Journal.

Why use the Three-by-Three Strategy Matrix?

The tool asks the question, "*Where do I want to be in three years?*". It shows the trade-offs between business, career and personal goals. Also, it challenges your rate of growth/development.

What is it?

Three by Three is a "*Where am I going? How am I going to get there?*" exercise. It looks at where you want to be in three years, and in one year, and asks, "*What do you need to do now?*". It looks at three distinct but interlocking aspects: your business, your career and your private life.

How to use it?

We recommend a minimum of 15 minutes to score yourself (see below). People who have been through similar exercises can often complete the initial run through in about 10. Next, reflect on what you have written. Finally, share and discuss the exercise with your partner if you feel comfortable doing that.

Instructions

Start writing in the boxes in the order you feel most comfortable. Ideally you will enter four to five bullet points in each box. Make the statements simple and try to put numbers in – or concrete things where possible. So, write "house worth £3m" rather than "big house", or "four-week African safari trip" rather than "big holiday". Make it real. Take, say, 15 minutes to fill in the matrix.

Ask yourself:

- "Where do I want the business to be in three years' time?"
- "So, where do I want the business to be in one year's time?"
- "So, what do I need to do now?"

And in turn:

- "Where do I want my professional life to be in three years' time?" "So, where do I want my professional life to be in one year's time?" "So, what do I need to do now?"
- "Where do I want my private life to be in three years' time?" "So, where do I want my private life to be in one year's time?" "So, what do I need to do now?"

Start with the end in mind

A large part of the strategy piece is debating and discussing where you want the business to be (and why).

Planning from where you are today is almost impossible... so many immediate things that need to be dealt with... so many small things that just aren't quite right.

However, if you start with the end in mind then it is much easier to map out the journey and the steps along the way.

Clarity about direction and trajectory is crucial. At the same time, you do need to work through the exercise, if only to make your mistakes on paper. If you are able to, you should spend at least a day a year stepping back and looking at where you want to be in three years' time.

Three-by-Three Matrix

FOR	THE BUSINESS	MY CAREER	MY PRIVATE LIFE
Where do you want to be in THREE years?	Part of the ownership of a successful growing business	Develop a strong and resilient and diverse business generating £600k+ per year in revenue	See my children reach full potential.
Where do you want to be in ONE year?	Have a clear strategy developed on how to reach the first objective.	Have fully explored all career opportunities and look to work with others on developing new cross opportunities.	Help each child to develop ideas about what they want to be.
What do you need to do NOW?	Develop plan not and buy-in from group on how we are going to achieve that	Develop business plan as a team.	Invest time in each child with time spent with them giving them confidence.

Three By Three was a big 'aha' for me. I needed to prioritise, now I have my life back!

—Cara Malone, Director

The Cascade exercise: Mapping the journey from vision to KPIs

Many consider the Cascade to be the meat of the business exercises. First you needed to understand "*where are you now?*" and consider where you wanted to be in the big picture format. Only then can you start to fill in the detail. It is this detail that you will be reflecting on in your weekly, monthly and quarterly progress in the Journal.

Why use the Cascade exercise?

Working through the process, top-down, creates a logical step-by-step process to underpin the what, why, when, where, who and how (WWWWWH) of all your business activities. It explains and justifies your business. It enables you to explain to yourself, your people and your customers exactly what you do and why. It makes sure there is a good fit and alignment between the higher and lower levels of your strategies and tactics.

What is it?

This is a "fill-in-the-boxes" exercise. The Cascade is a simple set of principles/ideas that interlink, starting with *purpose* then *vision, mission, strategy, milestones* and finishing with *key performance indicators*.

How to use it?

Starting at *Level 0 – Purpose*, work your way down the list taking up to, say, four lines to fill in each box. Each box is 'fed' by the previous box, e.g. if you deliver on your *Level 1 – Vision* then you should deliver on your *Level 0 – Purpose*.

To develop a working model of where you want to be requires creating a *Cascade* which helps you to clarify and define where you want to be. The value is in the thinking and discussion and not just the writing of the words.

It is a one-page exercise.

Do not get caught up in the various definitions of "*objectives*", "*purpose*", "*vision*"... everyone defines them differently. That's why we refer to them as Level 1, etc. It is the thinking that matters. Just accept our definitions or replace them with your own names.

The Cascade approach

We have worked with literally hundreds of boards. Robert's business specialises in delivering a boardroom process that consistently delivers actionable plans. We have honed down the strategy and planning process to several basics in a "strategy on a page" approach because, if you get the core fundamentals agreed and addressed, then everything else can come from that.

Values — part of your purpose

The piece that often gets businesses confused is the purpose part of the Cascade process. Many think that "purpose" is all about ethereal airy-fairy stuff of little relevance to a business. For some that may be true. However, time and time again, we see that a business without clarity about its values is like a ship sailing without a compass. The values tell you (and your people) what you stand for and what you believe in. Remove them and anything goes, which is a bad thing (unless of course that is your value statement!). So, top of the tree, top of the list to address, the thing that informs everything else, has to be your values.

Instructions

If you have recently gone through an effective strategy and business planning process, then you might be able to fill in the following worksheets in 10 minutes. It will be an interesting test to discover how much you remember or have bought into the various parts of the process.

Most people can work through the sheets in, say, an hour or so.

To give you an idea, we run half-day Cascade workshops where the majority of the sheets are thought through, worked through and filled in as first drafts.

Another option is to run a series of one- and two-hour workshops with your team (or by yourself!) where you reflect and consider your answers before you fill them in.

Our experience is that the first attempt at the exercise is often fairly accurate (although this is not the case when the business is facing extreme or especially challenging situations).

Start at *Level 0: Purpose* and slowly work your way through the sheets, reading the introduction to each part.

Numerous examples of full Cascades are available at the website **www.checkinjournal.com/thehub**.

Level 0: Purpose

 Working on our Purpose for the first time made us realise that we had never really discussed and debated what our core values really were. Quite terrifying. After some debate we felt much closer and more united about what was and was not acceptable. **"**

—Terry Walsh, Director

What are your values, purpose and niche? What is your reason for doing what you do? What is your "Why?" Why do you exist? What is your BHAG (Big Hairy Audacious Goal)? A BHAG is your ludicrously ambitious goal for, say, 10 years' time.

Your Purpose Questions

What are your values?

What is your purpose/cause/passion? Why do you do what you do?

What is the niche that you set out to serve?

What is your BHAG (Big Hairy Audacious Goal)?

Levels 1 & 2: Vision and Mission

 Despite being handed the usual 75-page corporate business plan, our business unit had never addressed how the disconnected targets we were given could make sense. Going back to basics and discovering our vision and mission (which fitted the corporate master plan) was a revelation. Finally our ducks were in a row!

—Jerry Cottle, UK Director

Fill in Level 1: Vision. What is your "blue skies" vision for the business? What does success look like in, say, three years? This is not about hard numbers but about what you want to be – e.g. to be known as, to be in the top three of, to be recognised as...

Then fill in Level 2: Mission. What are the numbers you want to hit (to achieve the vision) in, say, three years? For example, turnover, net profit, staff numbers, average transaction value, number of products, what you want to be.

Your Vision and Mission

Level 1: Vision. What do you want to be known for? What do you want to be famous for?

Level 2: Mission. What numbers do you want to hit in three years' time?

What will the business look and feel like when you hit these goals?

Level 3: Strategy

 We'd found the purpose, vision and mission discussions fascinating. Suddenly the strategy, how we were going to actually deliver on the numbers (the mission), needed to be articulated simply and succinctly. We struggled over this at first, but the resulting clarity of thinking meant we had something we could share with all the teams. Suddenly everyone understood what we were doing (and why). Amazing.

—Simon Woodcock, Founder-Director

Strategy

How we are going to do it: e.g. competing on price, competing on quality, best customer service, buying other businesses, hiring the best...

Level 3: Strategy. How are you going to make it happen?

Levels 4 & 5: Milestones and Key Performance Indicators

 I fancied myself as a bit of an expert at business planning, but the Check-in Journal process meant that itemising key milestones ahead became relatively easy. This time the right KPIs were generated – measuring the right stuff to achieve the milestones. Quick and simple. 🙲

—Toni Hancock, Managing Director

Level 4 is milestones or core success factors (CSFs). Steps on the way: e.g. 200th employee, new premises, hiring a BusDev Director, hitting 25% net profit...

Level 5: KPIs are key measures that matter: e.g. turnover, profit, cash, outstanding invoices, new clients, proposal conversion, complaints...

Milestones and KPIs

Level 4: Milestones

Level 5: Key Performance Indicators

As the list of key performance indicators (KPIs) suddenly gets out of hand, and as people recall the fear and trepidation that KPIs create, I ask you to trust us and go along with this particular process. While left in limbo for the moment, we will return (in Part 3) to create, focus and simplify the KPIs so that you can create a dashboard that you can use to run and monitor business performance.

Clients who use the dashboard process find that it makes everything simpler. It is a limited number of key metrics that focus on the achievement of your Vision, Mission and Strategy. They act like the lights in the airplane cockpit, feeding you the vital information that you need to be monitoring.

The Wallpaper exercise: Mapping out the journey ahead

Having mapped out the Cascade, which is a relatively logical, step-by-step process, this new exercise lets us test how the plans might roll-out. This is an examination of how things might take place. These plans will be translated into the goals and initiatives you will be monitoring and evaluating in your Journal.

Why use the Wallpaper exercise?

This visual exercise gets everyone involved and engaged. You can see the journey and the timeline and you can see the resource requirements and the outputs required. As a team exercise this creates buy-in and lively conversation and debate as the team map out how the various parts of the business will interconnect and work for each other.

What is it?

You literally take a roll of wallpaper. Lay it out across several tables (stick it down with masking tape). Map out a timeline and fill in where you are now and where you want to be in three years' time. Then fill in the gaps.

How to use it?

Once you have agreed the various parts of the Cascade, translate the words into a timeline chart. Use post-its or pencils and erasers so that nothing is final but can be moved and adjusted.

 The Wallpaper exercise was the meeting of minds for my senior management team and the board of trustees. It was where the words of the Cascade started to come to life. Everyone could see that things had to be in a certain order and that all initiatives were not equal. It forced us to prioritise and confront how we best use our scarce resources. We created the first plan that anyone really believed in! And now it's up on the wall for all to see.

—David Rouse, Finance Director

The best way to map out the Check-in Journal's *"Where are we now? Where are we going? How are we going to get there?"* exercises is to plot your path on a long piece of wallpaper – with the months written across the top from *"Today"* to *"Today +36 months"* – where you can start to piece together the targets and required resources as well as timings and order of work.

The Wallpaper exercise

Use a few metres of wallpaper or the template below. Plot current performance and three-year goals, then fill in the steps on the way. Here's an example followed by a blank template. For examples of the wallpaper exercise go to **www.checkinjournal.com/thehub**.

Instructions

1. Fill in key metrics for "Now"
2. Fill in key metrics for "+3y", where you want to be in three years' time
3. Fill in key activities on the timeline.

Top tip: If you use wallpaper, then use post-its to enter your goals and activities. If you are writing in the Journal, then use a pencil and eraser!

WALLPAPER–SAMPLE

NOW			+1Y		+2Y	+3Y
FINANCIALS	T/O	100	↑P	120	150	200
	NP.	10 (10%)		13.2 (11%)	18 (12%)	26 (13%)
	O/H	60 (60%)		70 (58%)	87 (58%)	114 (57%)
	d.cost	30 (30%)		36.8 (30%)	45 (30%)	60 (30%)
MARKETING	New Gold Clients	10	REBRAND	15	20	25
	Cost of Cust. Acquisition	5 k		5 k	5 k	5 k
	Cust. Lifetime Value	15 k	WEBSITE REVAMP	25 k	25 k	25 k
	Ave. Transaction Value	5 kpm		5 kpm	6 kpm	6 kpm
	Sales Team	5		6	7	8
OPERATIONS	Ops Team	25	FEB NEW PREMISES / JUNE OP-COSTS	26	37	38
PEOPLE	Head Count	45	JAN NEW HR DIR	50	68	70
	Board	4	FEB NEW H OF BUS	5	6	7
	Fred's role	MD	JUNE OPERATION OP CULTURE	MD	NEW MD CEO	RETIRED

32

WALLPAPER—SAMPLE

NOW	+1Y	+2Y	+3Y
FINANCIALS			
MARKETING			
OPERATIONS			
PEOPLE			

Government health warning

The creation of the Wallpaper is the start of a bigger process, a process that will make it easier to run and lead the business. A process that will help you to understand, agree, gain buy-in and achieve your goals faster and with less pain.

Imagining a vision for three years' time is more of an art than a science.

Who really knows how things will change for customers, competitors, the marketplace, the industry or in the political, economic, societal, technological, legislative and environmental worlds?

The Three-Year Goal is an aspiration, an articulation of the direction and rate of trajectory that you intend to follow. A way of making your mistakes on paper.

The reality is that having put together the big plan then you really need to focus on the next quarter, month, seven days and one day. It is all very well planning a great plane trip but first you have to get off the runway!

The generation and creation of the Wallpaper creates the key initiatives for the coming year.

Postscript

The materials and templates above are, to some extent, just the start of the business planning process. While it is not entirely necessary to create reams and reams of supporting reports, we have included some additional tools in Part 3 of the Journal. Use them if you feel they are appropriate for your situation. The documents in Part 3 are normally used as the next layer of supporting materials.

Remember: the purpose of the planning section of the Journal is to articulate exactly what it is that you are trying to do. The best way to do that is to clarify, simplify and focus on the key goals.

The Annual Business Plan

The final part of the business exercises is the business plan. Based on all your previous exercises, these are the numbers and initiatives that you will transfer into your Journal.

Why use the Annual Business Plan?

It puts all the key initiatives and goals on one page.

What is it?

This is a rough version of your plan for the business.

How to use it?

It is best to use the plan now, having gone through all of the earlier exercises.

So, where are we now? We have agreed or reflected on all the aspects of the plan for the business. We can concentrate all your work to date in the following Annual Business Plan.

Annual Business Plan

		YEAR ONE INITIATIVES			
			BUDGET	WHO	WHEN
PURPOSE	VALUES	FINANCIAL			
	PURPOSE/PASSION				
	NICHE				
	BHAG	MARKETING			
VISION	WANT TO BE KNOWN FOR:				
MISSION	NUMBERS:	OPERATIONS			
	THE BUSINESS WILL LOOK/FEEL				
STRATEGY	HOW WE'LL DO IT:				
		PEOPLE & CULTURE			
MILESTONES:					
PERFORMANCE INDICATORS		OTHER			

Personal Planning

This personal development section may appear to be shorter than the business section, but it is the part that most people find of most value. The reason for this is that many people are just too busy and don't have time to step back and review their progress.

Different people approach the personal planning differently. Horses for courses!

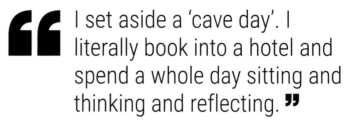

" I set aside a 'cave day'. I literally book into a hotel and spend a whole day sitting and thinking and reflecting. "

—David Storey, Director

" My best personal planning takes place when I am away from everything. A café in a foreign country or when I am stuck in a hotel room while working away from home. "

—Claudia Manzoni, IT Director

Probably Your Best Year Yet exercise: Identifying your roles and goals

The main exercise in the personal planning section is *Probably Your Best Year Yet*. If the Cascade is the heart of the business planning, then this is the heart of the personal planning and is the basis for all personal goals in the Journal.

Why use the Probably Your Best Year Yet exercise?

While most are happy to plan their business activity, few apply the same methodology to their private life. It makes sense to use a similar discipline. In fact, it is only when we get the business and the personal goals and actions all working together that things really become electric!

What is it?

We started the Check-in exercises with the Wheel of Life and the Three-by-Three Strategy Matrix, which got you to score your current "performance" and articulate your goals. (You may wish to revisit them.) This exercise challenges you to identify success and failure, your key roles and goals for your personal life, and prioritise accordingly. No small task.

How to use it?

This is a quiet room activity. You may need time. Quite a lot. There may be few questions and not a lot of paper, but this will get you really thinking.

The following worksheets address your recent successes and failures and are a great way to calibrate where you are and where you would like to focus your efforts over the coming year.

Go to www.checkinjournal.com/thehub to see examples and templates.

Probably Your Best Year Yet

Instructions: Spend some time alone and consider each question, one at a time. By the end you should have a list of actions that you need to carry out.

1. Looking back over your past year, what have been your *achievements*, and what have you learnt from these?

2. Looking back over your past year, what have been your *disappointments* (in other words, your failures), and what have you learnt from these?

3. What have been your *self-limiting beliefs*? What excuses have you made or used to justify poor performance? How will you overcome these?

Probably Your Best Year Yet (cont)

4. List your different roles in life – up to eight (e.g. father, husband, managing director, coach, boss).

5. For each role, list down eight things that you want to achieve in the coming year.

6. Which role is (or which roles are) most important to you? List your roles in order.

7. From the lists of all the goals for the forthcoming year, mark the eight most important ones.

Probably Your Best Year Yet (cont)

8. For the eight key goals, now address how you are going to achieve them. For each goal:
   - How will you know that you have achieved it?
   - What resources do you need?
   - When will you have completed it?
   - What others things is it dependent on?
   - What are the steps? Work out a timetable. Map your plan. This is a draft for your Annual Personal Plan (the next exercise).

Goal 1:

Goal 2:

Goal 3:

Goal 4:

Goal 5:

Goal 6:

Goal 7:

Goal 8:

9. Oh, and one more question! Which actions or behaviours have you used to (subconsciously) sabotage your previous efforts to succeed? What things might limit your success this time and how can you remove them?

The Annual Personal Plan

While many people have a business plan they work to, far fewer have a personal plan. You need to plan so you can measure and evaluate your progress towards your goals. Based on the previous Probably Your Best Year Yet work, you will keep returning to this in your Journal – either to remind yourself of what you set out to achieve or to revise your plans and goals.

Why use the Annual Personal Plan?

It puts all the key initiatives and goals on one page.

What is it?

This is your personal plan.

How to use it?

It is best to complete the plan now, having gone through all of the earlier exercises.

So, where are we now?

We have agreed or reflected on all the aspects of the plan for the business. And now we agree the annual personal plan.

Instructions:

Concentrate all your personal work to date in the following Annual Personal Plan.

Examples can be seen at **www.checkinjournal.com/ thehub**.

Annual Personal Plan

AREA/ACTIVITY	RESOURCES REQUIRED	COMPLETION INDICATOR	DEPENDS ON...	TIMETABLE. STEPS ON THE WAY...
1				
2				
3				
4				
5				
6				
7				
8				

Congratulations: you have now completed Part One, the exercises section. As you move to Part Two, the Journal, you will take all the work to date and apply it to Quarter 1 (Q1). Instructions are at the front of Part Two.

PART 2

THE JOURNAL

When you spend time working and reflecting on your daily goals it allows you to gain a sense of perspective and put your efforts into context. You also get the chance to align yourself against your vision, goals and objectives to truly understand if you are moving towards or away from what you are trying to achieve. What you wrote (or are still writing) in Part One can often seem a little remote. However, it is the small things you do on a daily basis that will change your habits and create new, better routines. Remember to recognise, to check off, what may seem like small victories on the way.

You've heard the saying,

 When eating an elephant take one bite at a time. **"**

—Creighton Abram

This is largely what the Journal is about.

 Successful journals break the deadlock of introspective obsession. **"**

—Alexandra Johnson

Using the Journal section

The pages in the Journal are in sequential order. The year is divided into four quarters and each quarter is divided into 13 weeks:

- At the start of each quarter, fill in your quarterly business plan and quarterly personal plan.

- At the start of each week, fill in your weekly preview and the weekly planning pages.
- At the end of each week, fill in the weekly review.
- At the end of each quarter, fill in the quarterly review, then go to the next quarterly business and personal plan.

Throughout the Journal we will prompt you to return to the exercises in Part One to make sure you are staying on track.

There is no one correct way to use the Journal. Different people will use it differently. However, the people who feel that they get the most out of the process are the ones that do the following:

1. Get into the habit of using the Journal on a regular basis, often at a regular time. Typically they set aside 15–30 minutes every Friday night (end of the work week) or Sunday night (reviewing the full week) or Monday morning (at the start of the new week).
2. The Journal is used to
   a. Review the last week
   b. Prepare for the coming week
   c. Reflect on how you have performed and what you could do better.
3. The Journal is also used to assess and re-assess the original goals and progress to date.
4. The time working on the Journal is often used as an interval of quiet time to reflect on how things are going.

Habits take some time to become established. In the early days, it may feel a little like you have to force yourself to commit the time to the process. However, the benefits (clarity, focus, reflection, results) become apparent very quickly.

Q1 Quarterly Business Plan

Instructions: This quarterly plan should be created by looking at the annual plan on page 35 and applying the relevant data to this quarter.

AREA/INITIATIVE	BUDGET	WHO	WHEN
FINANCIAL:			
MARKETING:			
OPERATIONS:			
PEOPLE:			
OTHER:			

Q1 Quarterly Personal Plan

Instructions: This quarterly plan should be created by looking at the annual personal plan on page 42 and applying the relevant data to this quarter.

AREA/INITIATIVE	OUTCOME	WHEN
FAMILY		
BUSINESS		
CAREER		
FUN		
SOCIAL		
HEALTH		
FINANCE		
WELLBEING/SPIRITUAL		

Weekly Preview, week 1

What is the weekly preview?

This is about taking stock and understanding the week that has just been and the week ahead.

Why use it?

We often take for granted and don't appreciate the steps we are taking towards our future. By understanding the focus for the coming week you become energised by the control you can have on moving your life forward.

How to use it?

We suggest a 15+ minute activity at the end of the week (Sunday night?) to give you clarity and allow you to start focusing on the week ahead.

Weekly Check-In Preview

Must do/urgent:

Must do/important:

Waiting/pending:

Delegate:

Carry forward:

1-CHECK: What's the *one* thing I *must* do this week (that will make other things easier or unnecessary):

1

3-CHECK: What are three projects/activities/actions that *must* be completed:

1

2

3

Weekly Planning, week 1

THIS WEEK'S BIG GOAL:

Monday

1 thing I must do:

3 actions/activities:

- ....
- ....
- ....

8
9
10
11
12
1
2
3
4
5
6
7
8

Tuesday

1 thing I must do:

3 actions/activities:

- ....
- ....
- ....

8
9
10
11
12
1
2
3
4
5
6
7
8

Wednesday

1 thing I must do:

3 actions/activities:

- ....
- ....
- ....

8
9
10
11
12
1
2
3
4
5
6
7
8

WHAT HAVE YOU DONE TOWARDS ACHIEVING YOUR WHEEL OF LIFE GOALS?

Family

Business

Career

Fun

THIS WEEK'S BIG TARGET:

Thursday	Friday	Saturday	Sunday
1 thing I must do:	**1 thing I must do:**	**1 thing I must do:**	**1 thing I must do:**
3 actions/activities:	3 actions/activities:	3 actions/activities:	3 actions/activities:

Thursday

1 thing I must do:

3 actions/activities:

- _____
- _____
- _____

8

9

10

11

12

1

2

3

4

5

6

7

8

Friday

1 thing I must do:

3 actions/activities:

- _____
- _____
- _____

8

9

10

11

12

1

2

3

4

5

6

7

8

Saturday

1 thing I must do:

3 actions/activities:

- _____
- _____
- _____

8

9

10

11

12

1

2

3

4

5

6

7

8

Sunday

1 thing I must do:

3 actions/activities:

- _____
- _____
- _____

8

9

10

11

12

1

2

3

4

5

6

7

8

Social

Health

Finance

Wellbeing/Spiritual

Who Had The Most Impact?

The Best Conversation?

What Inspired You?

How Were You Brave?

What Made You Happy?

One Word Summary

What Did You Avoid?

Best Moment?

Weekly Review, week 1

On a scale of 1–10, how has this week been?

What would +1 look like?

What has worked well this week?

This week would have been even better if...

What I gave to others is:

What I received from others is:

What I appreciated:

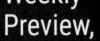

Weekly Preview, week 2

Weekly Check-In Preview

Must do/urgent:

Must do/important:

Waiting/pending:

Delegate:

Carry forward:

1-CHECK: What's the *one* thing I *must* do this week (that will make other things easier or unnecessary):

1

3-CHECK: What are three projects/activities/actions that *must* be completed:

1

2

3

Weekly Planning, week 2

THIS WEEK'S BIG GOAL:

Monday

1 thing I must do:

3 actions/activities:

- _____
- _____
- _____

8
9
10
11
12
1
2
3
4
5
6
7
8

Tuesday

1 thing I must do:

3 actions/activities:

- _____
- _____
- _____

8
9
10
11
12
1
2
3
4
5
6
7
8

Wednesday

1 thing I must do:

3 actions/activities:

- _____
- _____
- _____

8
9
10
11
12
1
2
3
4
5
6
7
8

WHAT HAVE YOU DONE TOWARDS ACHIEVING YOUR WHEEL OF LIFE GOALS?

Family

Business

Career

Fun

THIS WEEK'S BIG TARGET:

Thursday	Friday	Saturday	Sunday
1 thing I must do:	**1 thing I must do:**	**1 thing I must do:**	**1 thing I must do:**
3 actions/activities:	3 actions/activities:	3 actions/activities:	3 actions/activities:

Thursday
- ⋯
- ⋯
- ⋯

8
9
10
11
12
1
2
3
4
5
6
7
8

Friday
- ⋯
- ⋯
- ⋯

8
9
10
11
12
1
2
3
4
5
6
7
8

Saturday
- ⋯
- ⋯
- ⋯

8
9
10
11
12
1
2
3
4
5
6
7
8

Sunday
- ⋯
- ⋯
- ⋯

8
9
10
11
12
1
2
3
4
5
6
7
8

Social

Health

Finance

Wellbeing/Spiritual

Who Had The Most Impact?

The Best Conversation?

What Inspired You?

How Were You Brave?

What Made You Happy?

One Word Summary

What Did You Avoid?

Best Moment?

Weekly Review, week 2

On a scale of 1–10, how has this week been? ....

What would +1 look like? ....

What has worked well this week? ....

....

....

....

This week would have been even better if... ....

I love what I do because: ....

What do I need to start doing? ....

The elephant in the room that needs addressing is: ....

Weekly Preview, week 3

Weekly Check-In Preview

Must do/urgent:

Must do/important:

Waiting/pending:

Delegate:

Carry forward:

1-CHECK: What's the *one* thing I *must* do this week (that will make other things easier or unnecessary):

1

3-CHECK: What are three projects/activities/actions that *must* be completed:

1

2

3

Weekly Planning, week 3

THIS WEEK'S BIG GOAL:

Monday

1 thing I must do:

3 actions/activities:

-
-
-

8
9
10
11
12
1
2
3
4
5
6
7
8

Tuesday

1 thing I must do:

3 actions/activities:

-
-
-

8
9
10
11
12
1
2
3
4
5
6
7
8

Wednesday

1 thing I must do:

3 actions/activities:

-
-
-

8
9
10
11
12
1
2
3
4
5
6
7
8

**WHAT HAVE YOU DONE TOWARDS ACHIEVING
YOUR WHEEL OF LIFE GOALS?**

Family

Business

Career

Fun

THIS WEEK'S BIG TARGET:

Thursday

1 thing I must do:

3 actions/activities:

- ....
- ....
- ....

8 ....
9 ....
10 ....
11 ....
12 ....
1 ....
2 ....
3 ....
4 ....
5 ....
6 ....
7 ....
8 ....

Friday

1 thing I must do:

3 actions/activities:

- ....
- ....
- ....

8 ....
9 ....
10 ....
11 ....
12 ....
1 ....
2 ....
3 ....
4 ....
5 ....
6 ....
7 ....
8 ....

Saturday

1 thing I must do:

3 actions/activities:

- ....
- ....
- ....

8 ....
9 ....
10 ....
11 ....
12 ....
1 ....
2 ....
3 ....
4 ....
5 ....
6 ....
7 ....
8 ....

Sunday

1 thing I must do:

3 actions/activities:

- ....
- ....
- ....

8 ....
9 ....
10 ....
11 ....
12 ....
1 ....
2 ....
3 ....
4 ....
5 ....
6 ....
7 ....
8 ....

Social

Health

Finance

Wellbeing/Spiritual

Who Had The Most Impact?

The Best Conversation?

What Inspired You?

How Were You Brave?

What Made You Happy?

One Word Summary

What Did You Avoid?

Best Moment?

Weekly Review, week 3

On a scale of 1–10, how has this week been? ....

What would +1 look like? ....

What has worked well this week? ....

....

....

....

This week would have been even better if… ....

Where's the focus? ....

The most important upcoming meeting is: ....

What do I need to change and why? ....

Weekly Preview, week 4

Weekly Check-In Preview

Must do/urgent:

Must do/important:

Waiting/pending:

Delegate:

Carry forward:

1-CHECK: What's the *one* thing I *must* do this week (that will make other things easier or unnecessary):

1

3-CHECK: What are three projects/activities/actions that *must* be completed:

1

2

3

Weekly Planning, week 4

THIS WEEK'S BIG GOAL:

Monday	Tuesday	Wednesday
1 thing I must do:	**1 thing I must do:**	**1 thing I must do:**
3 actions/activities:	3 actions/activities:	3 actions/activities:

Monday

-
-
-

8
9
10
11
12
1
2
3
4
5
6
7
8

Tuesday

-
-
-

8
9
10
11
12
1
2
3
4
5
6
7
8

Wednesday

-
-
-

8
9
10
11
12
1
2
3
4
5
6
7
8

WHAT HAVE YOU DONE TOWARDS ACHIEVING YOUR WHEEL OF LIFE GOALS?

Family

Business

Career

Fun

THIS WEEK'S BIG TARGET:

Thursday	Friday	Saturday	Sunday

1 thing I must do:

3 actions/activities:

- ⚫ ....
- ⚫ ....
- ⚫ ....

8
9
10
11
12
1
2
3
4
5
6
7
8

1 thing I must do:

3 actions/activities:

- ⚫ ....
- ⚫ ....
- ⚫ ....

8
9
10
11
12
1
2
3
4
5
6
7
8

1 thing I must do:

3 actions/activities:

- ⚫ ....
- ⚫ ....
- ⚫ ....

8
9
10
11
12
1
2
3
4
5
6
7
8

1 thing I must do:

3 actions/activities:

- ⚫ ....
- ⚫ ....
- ⚫ ....

8
9
10
11
12
1
2
3
4
5
6
7
8

Social	Who Had The Most Impact?	What Made You Happy?
Health	The Best Conversation?	One Word Summary
Finance	What Inspired You?	What Did You Avoid?
Wellbeing/Spiritual	How Were You Brave?	Best Moment?

Weekly Review, week 4

On a scale of 1–10, how has this week been? ....

What would +1 look like? ....

What has worked well this week? ....

....

....

....

This week would have been even better if... ....

Who do I need to thank and why? ....

One conversation I need to have: ....

What's holding me back? ....

Weekly Preview, week 5

Weekly Check-In Preview

Must do/urgent:

Must do/important:

Waiting/pending:

Delegate:

Carry forward:

1-CHECK: What's the *one* thing I *must* do this week (that will make other things easier or unnecessary):

1

3-CHECK: What are three projects/activities/actions that *must* be completed:

1

2

3

Weekly Planning, week 5

THIS WEEK'S BIG GOAL:

Monday	Tuesday	Wednesday
1 thing I must do:	**1 thing I must do:**	**1 thing I must do:**
3 actions/activities:	3 actions/activities:	3 actions/activities:

Monday

1 thing I must do:

3 actions/activities:

-
-
-

8

9

10

11

12

1

2

3

4

5

6

7

8

Tuesday

1 thing I must do:

3 actions/activities:

-
-
-

8

9

10

11

12

1

2

3

4

5

6

7

8

Wednesday

1 thing I must do:

3 actions/activities:

-
-
-

8

9

10

11

12

1

2

3

4

5

6

7

8

WHAT HAVE YOU DONE TOWARDS ACHIEVING YOUR WHEEL OF LIFE GOALS?

Family

Business

Career

Fun

THIS WEEK'S BIG TARGET:

Thursday	Friday	Saturday	Sunday

Thursday

1 thing I must do:

3 actions/activities:

- ....
- ....
- ....

8

9

10

11

12

1

2

3

4

5

6

7

8

Friday

1 thing I must do:

3 actions/activities:

- ....
- ....
- ....

8

9

10

11

12

1

2

3

4

5

6

7

8

Saturday

1 thing I must do:

3 actions/activities:

- ....
- ....
- ....

8

9

10

11

12

1

2

3

4

5

6

7

8

Sunday

1 thing I must do:

3 actions/activities:

- ....
- ....
- ....

8

9

10

11

12

1

2

3

4

5

6

7

8

Social

Health

Finance

Wellbeing/Spiritual

Who Had The Most Impact?

The Best Conversation?

What Inspired You?

How Were You Brave?

What Made You Happy?

One Word Summary

What Did You Avoid?

Best Moment?

Weekly Review, week 5

On a scale of 1–10, how has this week been? ....

What would +1 look like? ....

What has worked well this week? ....

....

....

....

....

This week would have been even better if... ....

What I gave to others is: ....

What I received from others is: ....

What I appreciated: ....

Weekly Preview, week 6

Weekly Check-In Preview

Must do/urgent:

Must do/important:

Waiting/pending:

Delegate:

Carry forward:

1-CHECK: What's the *one* thing I *must* do this week (that will make other things easier or unnecessary):

1

3-CHECK: What are three projects/activities/actions that *must* be completed:

1

2

3

Weekly Planning, week 6

THIS WEEK'S BIG GOAL:

Monday

1 thing I must do:

3 actions/activities:

- ....
- ....
- ....

8
9
10
11
12
1
2
3
4
5
6
7
8

Tuesday

1 thing I must do:

3 actions/activities:

- ....
- ....
- ....

8
9
10
11
12
1
2
3
4
5
6
7
8

Wednesday

1 thing I must do:

3 actions/activities:

- ....
- ....
- ....

8
9
10
11
12
1
2
3
4
5
6
7
8

WHAT HAVE YOU DONE TOWARDS ACHIEVING YOUR WHEEL OF LIFE GOALS?

Family

Business

Career

Fun

THIS WEEK'S BIG TARGET:

Thursday

1 thing I must do:

3 actions/activities:

- ●
- ●
- ●

8

9

10

11

12

1

2

3

4

5

6

7

8

Friday

1 thing I must do:

3 actions/activities:

- ●
- ●
- ●

8

9

10

11

12

1

2

3

4

5

6

7

8

Saturday

1 thing I must do:

3 actions/activities:

- ●
- ●
- ●

8

9

10

11

12

1

2

3

4

5

6

7

8

Sunday

1 thing I must do:

3 actions/activities:

- ●
- ●
- ●

8

9

10

11

12

1

2

3

4

5

6

7

8

Social

Health

Finance

Wellbeing/Spiritual

Who Had The Most Impact?

The Best Conversation?

What Inspired You?

How Were You Brave?

What Made You Happy?

One Word Summary

What Did You Avoid?

Best Moment?

Weekly Review, week 6

On a scale of 1–10, how has this week been?

What would +1 look like?

What has worked well this week?

This week would have been even better if…

I love what I do because:

What do I need to start doing?

The elephant in the room that needs addressing is:

Weekly Preview, week 7

Weekly Check-In Preview

Must do/urgent:

Must do/important:

Waiting/pending:

Delegate:

Carry forward:

1-CHECK: What's the *one* thing I *must* do this week (that will make other things easier or unnecessary):

1

3-CHECK: What are three projects/activities/actions that *must* be completed:

1

2

3

Weekly Planning, week 7

THIS WEEK'S BIG GOAL:

Monday

1 thing I must do:

3 actions/activities:

- ....
- ....
- ....

8 ....
9 ....
10 ....
11 ....
12 ....
1 ....
2 ....
3 ....
4 ....
5 ....
6 ....
7 ....
8 ....

Tuesday

1 thing I must do:

3 actions/activities:

- ....
- ....
- ....

8 ....
9 ....
10 ....
11 ....
12 ....
1 ....
2 ....
3 ....
4 ....
5 ....
6 ....
7 ....
8 ....

Wednesday

1 thing I must do:

3 actions/activities:

- ....
- ....
- ....

8 ....
9 ....
10 ....
11 ....
12 ....
1 ....
2 ....
3 ....
4 ....
5 ....
6 ....
7 ....
8 ....

WHAT HAVE YOU DONE TOWARDS ACHIEVING YOUR WHEEL OF LIFE GOALS?

Family

Business

Career

Fun

THIS WEEK'S BIG TARGET:

Thursday	Friday	Saturday	Sunday

1 thing I must do:

3 actions/activities:

-
-
-

8

9

10

11

12

1

2

3

4

5

6

7

8

Social

Health

Finance

Wellbeing/Spiritual

Who Had The Most Impact?

The Best Conversation?

What Inspired You?

How Were You Brave?

What Made You Happy?

One Word Summary

What Did You Avoid?

Best Moment?

Weekly Review, week 7

On a scale of 1–10, how has this week been?

What would +1 look like?

What has worked well this week?

This week would have been even better if…

Where's the focus?

The most important upcoming meeting is:

What do I need to change and why?

Weekly Preview, week 8

Weekly Check-In Preview

Must do/urgent:

Must do/important:

Waiting/pending:

Delegate:

Carry forward:

1-CHECK: What's the *one* thing I *must* do this week (that will make other things easier or unnecessary):

1

3-CHECK: What are three projects/activities/actions that *must* be completed:

1

2

3

Weekly Planning, week 8

Monday

1 thing I must do:

3 actions/activities:

- ·
- ·
- ·

8

9

10

11

12

1

2

3

4

5

6

7

8

Tuesday

1 thing I must do:

3 actions/activities:

- ·
- ·
- ·

8

9

10

11

12

1

2

3

4

5

6

7

8

Wednesday

1 thing I must do:

3 actions/activities:

- ·
- ·
- ·

8

9

10

11

12

1

2

3

4

5

6

7

8

WHAT HAVE YOU DONE TOWARDS ACHIEVING YOUR WHEEL OF LIFE GOALS?

Family

Business

Career

Fun

THIS WEEK'S BIG TARGET:

Thursday	Friday	Saturday	Sunday

1 thing I must do:

3 actions/activities:

-
-
-

8

9

10

11

12

1

2

3

4

5

6

7

8

Social

Health

Finance

Wellbeing/Spiritual

Who Had The Most Impact?

The Best Conversation?

What Inspired You?

How Were You Brave?

What Made You Happy?

One Word Summary

What Did You Avoid?

Best Moment?

Weekly Review, week 8

On a scale of 1–10, how has this week been?

What would +1 look like?

What has worked well this week?

This week would have been even better if…

Who do I need to thank and why?

One conversation I need to have:

What's holding me back?

Weekly Preview, week 9

Must do/urgent:

Must do/important:

Waiting/pending:

Delegate:

Carry forward:

1-CHECK: What's the *one* thing I *must* do this week (that will make other things easier or unnecessary):

1

3-CHECK: What are three projects/activities/actions that *must* be completed:

1

2

3

Weekly Planning, week 9

Monday

1 thing I must do:

3 actions/activities:

- ....
- ....
- ....

8

9

10

11

12

1

2

3

4

5

6

7

8

Tuesday

1 thing I must do:

3 actions/activities:

- ....
- ....
- ....

8

9

10

11

12

1

2

3

4

5

6

7

8

Wednesday

1 thing I must do:

3 actions/activities:

- ....
- ....
- ....

8

9

10

11

12

1

2

3

4

5

6

7

8

WHAT HAVE YOU DONE TOWARDS ACHIEVING YOUR WHEEL OF LIFE GOALS?

Family

Business

Career

Fun

THIS WEEK'S BIG TARGET:

Thursday	Friday	Saturday	Sunday

1 thing I must do:

3 actions/activities:

-
-
-

8

9

10

11

12

1

2

3

4

5

6

7

8

Social

Health

Finance

Wellbeing/Spiritual

Who Had The Most Impact?

The Best Conversation?

What Inspired You?

How Were You Brave?

What Made You Happy?

One Word Summary

What Did You Avoid?

Best Moment?

Weekly Review, week 9

On a scale of 1–10, how has this week been? ....

What would +1 look like? ....

What has worked well this week? ....

....

....

....

This week would have been even better if... ....

What I gave to others is: ....

What I received from others is: ....

What I appreciated: ....

Weekly Preview, week 10

Weekly Check-In Preview

Must do/urgent:

Must do/important:

Waiting/pending:

Delegate:

Carry forward:

1-CHECK: What's the *one* thing I *must* do this week (that will make other things easier or unnecessary):

1

3-CHECK: What are three projects/activities/actions that *must* be completed:

1

2

3

Weekly Planning, week 10

THIS WEEK'S BIG GOAL:

Monday

1 thing I must do:

3 actions/activities:

-
-
-

8

9

10

11

12

1

2

3

4

5

6

7

8

Tuesday

1 thing I must do:

3 actions/activities:

-
-
-

8

9

10

11

12

1

2

3

4

5

6

7

8

Wednesday

1 thing I must do:

3 actions/activities:

-
-
-

8

9

10

11

12

1

2

3

4

5

6

7

8

WHAT HAVE YOU DONE TOWARDS ACHIEVING YOUR WHEEL OF LIFE GOALS?

Family

Business

Career

Fun

THIS WEEK'S BIG TARGET:

Thursday	Friday	Saturday	Sunday

Thursday

1 thing I must do:

3 actions/activities:

- ....
- ....
- ....

8
9
10
11
12
1
2
3
4
5
6
7
8

Friday

1 thing I must do:

3 actions/activities:

- ....
- ....
- ....

8
9
10
11
12
1
2
3
4
5
6
7
8

Saturday

1 thing I must do:

3 actions/activities:

- ....
- ....
- ....

8
9
10
11
12
1
2
3
4
5
6
7
8

Sunday

1 thing I must do:

3 actions/activities:

- ....
- ....
- ....

8
9
10
11
12
1
2
3
4
5
6
7
8

Social

Health

Finance

Wellbeing/Spiritual

Who Had The Most Impact?

The Best Conversation?

What Inspired You?

How Were You Brave?

What Made You Happy?

One Word Summary

What Did You Avoid?

Best Moment?

Weekly Review, week 10

On a scale of 1–10, how has this week been?

What would +1 look like?

What has worked well this week?

This week would have been even better if…

I love what I do because:

What do I need to start doing?

The elephant in the room that needs addressing is:

Weekly Preview, week 11

Weekly Check-In Preview

Must do/urgent:

Must do/important:

Waiting/pending:

Delegate:

Carry forward:

1-CHECK: What's the *one* thing I *must* do this week (that will make other things easier or unnecessary):

1

3-CHECK: What are three projects/activities/actions that *must* be completed:

1

2

3

Weekly Planning, week 11

THIS WEEK'S BIG GOAL:

Monday

1 thing I must do:

3 actions/activities:

-
-
-

8

9

10

11

12

1

2

3

4

5

6

7

8

Tuesday

1 thing I must do:

3 actions/activities:

-
-
-

8

9

10

11

12

1

2

3

4

5

6

7

8

Wednesday

1 thing I must do:

3 actions/activities:

-
-
-

8

9

10

11

12

1

2

3

4

5

6

7

8

WHAT HAVE YOU DONE TOWARDS ACHIEVING YOUR WHEEL OF LIFE GOALS?

Family

Business

Career

Fun

THIS WEEK'S BIG TARGET:

Thursday

1 thing I must do:

3 actions/activities:

-
-
-

8

9

10

11

12

1

2

3

4

5

6

7

8

Friday

1 thing I must do:

3 actions/activities:

-
-
-

8

9

10

11

12

1

2

3

4

5

6

7

8

Saturday

1 thing I must do:

3 actions/activities:

-
-
-

8

9

10

11

12

1

2

3

4

5

6

7

8

Sunday

1 thing I must do:

3 actions/activities:

-
-
-

8

9

10

11

12

1

2

3

4

5

6

7

8

Social

Health

Finance

Wellbeing/Spiritual

Who Had The Most Impact?

The Best Conversation?

What Inspired You?

How Were You Brave?

What Made You Happy?

One Word Summary

What Did You Avoid?

Best Moment?

Weekly Review, week 11

On a scale of 1–10, how has this week been?

What would +1 look like?

What has worked well this week?

This week would have been even better if…

Where's the focus?

The most important upcoming meeting is:

What do I need to change and why?

Weekly Preview, week 12

Weekly Check-In Preview

Must do/urgent:

Must do/important:

Waiting/pending:

Delegate:

Carry forward:

1-CHECK: What's the *one* thing I *must* do this week (that will make other things easier or unnecessary):

1

3-CHECK: What are three projects/activities/actions that *must* be completed:

1

2

3

Weekly Planning, week 12

Monday

1 thing I must do:

3 actions/activities:

- ....
- ....
- ....

8

9

10

11

12

1

2

3

4

5

6

7

8

Tuesday

1 thing I must do:

3 actions/activities:

- ....
- ....
- ....

8

9

10

11

12

1

2

3

4

5

6

7

8

Wednesday

1 thing I must do:

3 actions/activities:

- ....
- ....
- ....

8

9

10

11

12

1

2

3

4

5

6

7

8

WHAT HAVE YOU DONE TOWARDS ACHIEVING YOUR WHEEL OF LIFE GOALS?

Family

Business

Career

Fun

THIS WEEK'S BIG TARGET:

Thursday	Friday	Saturday	Sunday

1 thing I must do:

3 actions/activities:

- ....
- ....
- ....

1 thing I must do:

3 actions/activities:

- ....
- ....
- ....

1 thing I must do:

3 actions/activities:

- ....
- ....
- ....

1 thing I must do:

3 actions/activities:

- ....
- ....
- ....

Thursday	Friday	Saturday	Sunday
8	8	8	8
9	9	9	9
10	10	10	10
11	11	11	11
12	12	12	12
1	1	1	1
2	2	2	2
3	3	3	3
4	4	4	4
5	5	5	5
6	6	6	6
7	7	7	7
8	8	8	8

Social

Health

Finance

Wellbeing/Spiritual

Who Had The Most Impact?

The Best Conversation?

What Inspired You?

How Were You Brave?

What Made You Happy?

One Word Summary

What Did You Avoid?

Best Moment?

Weekly Review, week 12

On a scale of 1–10, how has this week been? ....

What would +1 look like? ....

What has worked well this week? ....

....

....

....

....

This week would have been even better if... ....

Who do I need to thank and why? ....

One conversation I need to have: ....

What's holding me back? ....

Weekly Preview, week 13

Weekly Check-In Preview

Must do/urgent:

Must do/important:

Waiting/pending:

Delegate:

Carry forward:

1-CHECK: What's the *one* thing I *must* do this week (that will make other things easier or unnecessary):

1

3-CHECK: What are three projects/activities/actions that *must* be completed:

1

2

3

Weekly Planning, week 13

THIS WEEK'S BIG GOAL:

Monday

1 thing I must do:

3 actions/activities:

- ....
- ....
- ....

8 ....
9 ....
10 ....
11 ....
12 ....
1 ....
2 ....
3 ....
4 ....
5 ....
6 ....
7 ....
8 ....

Tuesday

1 thing I must do:

3 actions/activities:

- ....
- ....
- ....

8 ....
9 ....
10 ....
11 ....
12 ....
1 ....
2 ....
3 ....
4 ....
5 ....
6 ....
7 ....
8 ....

Wednesday

1 thing I must do:

3 actions/activities:

- ....
- ....
- ....

8 ....
9 ....
10 ....
11 ....
12 ....
1 ....
2 ....
3 ....
4 ....
5 ....
6 ....
7 ....
8 ....

WHAT HAVE YOU DONE TOWARDS ACHIEVING YOUR WHEEL OF LIFE GOALS?

Family

Business

Career

Fun

THIS WEEK'S BIG TARGET:

Thursday	Friday	Saturday	Sunday

1 thing I must do:

3 actions/activities:

-
-
-

8

9

10

11

12

1

2

3

4

5

6

7

8

---

1 thing I must do:

3 actions/activities:

-
-
-

8

9

10

11

12

1

2

3

4

5

6

7

8

---

1 thing I must do:

3 actions/activities:

-
-
-

8

9

10

11

12

1

2

3

4

5

6

7

8

---

1 thing I must do:

3 actions/activities:

-
-
-

8

9

10

11

12

1

2

3

4

5

6

7

8

Social

Health

Finance

Wellbeing/Spiritual

Who Had The Most Impact?

The Best Conversation?

What Inspired You?

How Were You Brave?

What Made You Happy?

One Word Summary

What Did You Avoid?

Best Moment?

Weekly Review, week 13

On a scale of 1–10, how has this week been?

What would +1 look like?

What has worked well this week?

This week would have been even better if…

As we approach the end of the quarter, what have you failed to do?

What do you need to check?

Who do you still need to contact?

Q1 Quarterly Review

What do you feel were your most significant accomplishments?

Professional/Business: ....

Personal/Family: ....

What do you feel were your most significant disappointments?

Professional/Business: ....

Personal/Family: ....

Q1 Quarterly Business Review

AREA/INITIATIVE	SCORE OUT OF 10	WHY
FINANCIAL:		
MARKETING:		
OPERATIONS:		
PEOPLE & CULTURE:		
OTHER:		

Q1
Quarterly
Personal
Review

AREA/INITIATIVE	SCORE OUT OF 10	WHY
FAMILY		
BUSINESS		
CAREER		
FUN		
SOCIAL		
HEALTH		
FINANCE		
WELLBEING/SPIRITUAL		

NOTES

NOTES

NOTES

Q2 Quarterly Business Plan

Instructions: This quarterly plan should be created by looking at the annual plan on page 35 and applying the relevant data to this quarter.

AREA/INITIATIVE	BUDGET	WHO	WHEN
FINANCIAL:			
MARKETING:			
OPERATIONS:			
PEOPLE:			
OTHER:			

Q2 Quarterly Personal Plan

Instructions: This quarterly plan should be created by looking at the annual personal plan on page 42 and applying the relevant data to this quarter.

AREA/INITIATIVE	OUTCOME	WHEN
FAMILY		
BUSINESS		
CAREER		
FUN		
SOCIAL		
HEALTH		
FINANCE		
WELLBEING/SPIRITUAL		

Weekly Preview, week 1

Weekly Check-In Preview

Must do/urgent:

Must do/important:

Waiting/pending:

Delegate:

Carry forward:

1-CHECK: What's the *one* thing I *must* do this week (that will make other things easier or unnecessary):

1

3-CHECK: What are three projects/activities/actions that *must* be completed:

1

2

3

Weekly Planning, week 1

THIS WEEK'S BIG GOAL:

Monday

1 thing I must do:

3 actions/activities:

- ....
- ....
- ....

8
9
10
11
12
1
2
3
4
5
6
7
8

Tuesday

1 thing I must do:

3 actions/activities:

- ....
- ....
- ....

8
9
10
11
12
1
2
3
4
5
6
7
8

Wednesday

1 thing I must do:

3 actions/activities:

- ....
- ....
- ....

8
9
10
11
12
1
2
3
4
5
6
7
8

WHAT HAVE YOU DONE TOWARDS ACHIEVING YOUR WHEEL OF LIFE GOALS?

Family

Business

Career

Fun

THIS WEEK'S BIG TARGET:

Thursday

1 thing I must do:

3 actions/activities:

-
-
-

8

9

10

11

12

1

2

3

4

5

6

7

8

Friday

1 thing I must do:

3 actions/activities:

-
-
-

8

9

10

11

12

1

2

3

4

5

6

7

8

Saturday

1 thing I must do:

3 actions/activities:

-
-
-

8

9

10

11

12

1

2

3

4

5

6

7

8

Sunday

1 thing I must do:

3 actions/activities:

-
-
-

8

9

10

11

12

1

2

3

4

5

6

7

8

Social

Health

Finance

Wellbeing/Spiritual

Who Had The Most Impact?

The Best Conversation?

What Inspired You?

How Were You Brave?

What Made You Happy?

One Word Summary

What Did You Avoid?

Best Moment?

Weekly Review, week 1

On a scale of 1–10, how has this week been?

What would +1 look like?

What has worked well this week?

This week would have been even better if...

What I gave to others is:

What I received from others is:

What I appreciated:

Weekly Preview, week 2

Weekly Check-In Preview

Must do/urgent:

Must do/important:

Waiting/pending:

Delegate:

Carry forward:

1-CHECK: What's the *one* thing I *must* do this week (that will make other things easier or unnecessary):

1

3-CHECK: What are three projects/activities/actions that *must* be completed:

1

2

3

Weekly Planning, week 2

THIS WEEK'S BIG GOAL:

Monday

1 thing I must do:

3 actions/activities:

- ·
- ·
- ·

8
9
10
11
12
1
2
3
4
5
6
7
8

Tuesday

1 thing I must do:

3 actions/activities:

- ·
- ·
- ·

8
9
10
11
12
1
2
3
4
5
6
7
8

Wednesday

1 thing I must do:

3 actions/activities:

- ·
- ·
- ·

8
9
10
11
12
1
2
3
4
5
6
7
8

WHAT HAVE YOU DONE TOWARDS ACHIEVING YOUR WHEEL OF LIFE GOALS?

Family

Business

Career

Fun

THIS WEEK'S BIG TARGET:

Thursday

1 thing I must do:

3 actions/activities:

- ....
- ....
- ....

8
9
10
11
12
1
2
3
4
5
6
7
8

Friday

1 thing I must do:

3 actions/activities:

- ....
- ....
- ....

8
9
10
11
12
1
2
3
4
5
6
7
8

Saturday

1 thing I must do:

3 actions/activities:

- ....
- ....
- ....

8
9
10
11
12
1
2
3
4
5
6
7
8

Sunday

1 thing I must do:

3 actions/activities:

- ....
- ....
- ....

8
9
10
11
12
1
2
3
4
5
6
7
8

Social

Health

Finance

Wellbeing/Spiritual

Who Had The Most Impact?

The Best Conversation?

What Inspired You?

How Were You Brave?

What Made You Happy?

One Word Summary

What Did You Avoid?

Best Moment?

Weekly Review, week 2

On a scale of 1–10, how has this week been? ....

What would +1 look like? ....

What has worked well this week? ....

....

....

....

....

This week would have been even better if... ....

I love what I do because: ....

What do I need to start doing? ....

The elephant in the room that needs addressing is: ....

Weekly Preview, week 3

Weekly Check-In Preview

Must do/urgent:

Must do/important:

Waiting/pending:

Delegate:

Carry forward:

1-CHECK: What's the *one* thing I *must* do this week (that will make other things easier or unnecessary):

1

3-CHECK: What are three projects/activities/actions that *must* be completed:

1

2

3

Weekly Planning, week 3

THIS WEEK'S BIG GOAL:

Monday

1 thing I must do:

3 actions/activities:

- ....
- ....
- ....

8

9

10

11

12

1

2

3

4

5

6

7

8

Tuesday

1 thing I must do:

3 actions/activities:

- ....
- ....
- ....

8

9

10

11

12

1

2

3

4

5

6

7

8

Wednesday

1 thing I must do:

3 actions/activities:

- ....
- ....
- ....

8

9

10

11

12

1

2

3

4

5

6

7

8

WHAT HAVE YOU DONE TOWARDS ACHIEVING YOUR WHEEL OF LIFE GOALS?

Family

Business

Career

Fun

THIS WEEK'S BIG TARGET:

Thursday

1 thing I must do:

3 actions/activities:

- ....
- ....
- ....

8

9

10

11

12

1

2

3

4

5

6

7

8

Friday

1 thing I must do:

3 actions/activities:

- ....
- ....
- ....

8

9

10

11

12

1

2

3

4

5

6

7

8

Saturday

1 thing I must do:

3 actions/activities:

- ....
- ....
- ....

8

9

10

11

12

1

2

3

4

5

6

7

8

Sunday

1 thing I must do:

3 actions/activities:

- ....
- ....
- ....

8

9

10

11

12

1

2

3

4

5

6

7

8

Social

Health

Finance

Wellbeing/Spiritual

Who Had The Most Impact?

The Best Conversation?

What Inspired You?

How Were You Brave?

What Made You Happy?

One Word Summary

What Did You Avoid?

Best Moment?

Weekly Review, week 3

On a scale of 1–10, how has this week been?

What would +1 look like?

What has worked well this week?

This week would have been even better if...

Where's the focus?

The most important upcoming meeting is:

What do I need to change and why?

Weekly Preview, week 4

Must do/urgent:

Must do/important:

Waiting/pending:

Delegate:

Carry forward:

1-CHECK: What's the *one* thing I *must* do this week (that will make other things easier or unnecessary):

1

3-CHECK: What are three projects/activities/actions that *must* be completed:

1

2

3

Weekly Planning, week 4

THIS WEEK'S BIG GOAL:

Monday

1 thing I must do:

3 actions/activities:

- ....
- ....
- ....

8
9
10
11
12
1
2
3
4
5
6
7
8

Tuesday

1 thing I must do:

3 actions/activities:

- ....
- ....
- ....

8
9
10
11
12
1
2
3
4
5
6
7
8

Wednesday

1 thing I must do:

3 actions/activities:

- ....
- ....
- ....

8
9
10
11
12
1
2
3
4
5
6
7
8

WHAT HAVE YOU DONE TOWARDS ACHIEVING YOUR WHEEL OF LIFE GOALS?

Family

Business

Career

Fun

THIS WEEK'S BIG TARGET:

| Thursday | Friday | Saturday | Sunday |

Thursday

1 thing I must do:

3 actions/activities:

- ....
- ....
- ....

8 ....

9 ....

10 ....

11 ....

12 ....

1 ....

2 ....

3 ....

4 ....

5 ....

6 ....

7 ....

8 ....

Friday

1 thing I must do:

3 actions/activities:

- ....
- ....
- ....

8 ....

9 ....

10 ....

11 ....

12 ....

1 ....

2 ....

3 ....

4 ....

5 ....

6 ....

7 ....

8 ....

Saturday

1 thing I must do:

3 actions/activities:

- ....
- ....
- ....

8 ....

9 ....

10 ....

11 ....

12 ....

1 ....

2 ....

3 ....

4 ....

5 ....

6 ....

7 ....

8 ....

Sunday

1 thing I must do:

3 actions/activities:

- ....
- ....
- ....

8 ....

9 ....

10 ....

11 ....

12 ....

1 ....

2 ....

3 ....

4 ....

5 ....

6 ....

7 ....

8 ....

Social

Health

Finance

Wellbeing/Spiritual

Who Had The Most Impact?

The Best Conversation?

What Inspired You?

How Were You Brave?

What Made You Happy?

One Word Summary

What Did You Avoid?

Best Moment?

Weekly Review, week 4

On a scale of 1–10, how has this week been? ....

What would +1 look like? ....

What has worked well this week? ....

....

....

....

....

This week would have been even better if... ....

Who do I need to thank and why? ....

One conversation I need to have: ....

What's holding me back? ....

Weekly Preview, week 5

Weekly Check-In Preview

Must do/urgent:

Must do/important:

Waiting/pending:

Delegate:

Carry forward:

1-CHECK: What's the *one* thing I *must* do this week (that will make other things easier or unnecessary):

1

3-CHECK: What are three projects/activities/actions that *must* be completed:

1

2

3

Weekly Planning, week 5

THIS WEEK'S BIG GOAL:

Monday

1 thing I must do:

3 actions/activities:

- ....
- ....
- ....

8

9

10

11

12

1

2

3

4

5

6

7

8

Tuesday

1 thing I must do:

3 actions/activities:

- ....
- ....
- ....

8

9

10

11

12

1

2

3

4

5

6

7

8

Wednesday

1 thing I must do:

3 actions/activities:

- ....
- ....
- ....

8

9

10

11

12

1

2

3

4

5

6

7

8

WHAT HAVE YOU DONE TOWARDS ACHIEVING YOUR WHEEL OF LIFE GOALS?

Family

Business

Career

Fun

THIS WEEK'S BIG TARGET:

Thursday

1 thing I must do:

3 actions/activities:

- ....
- ....
- ....

8
9
10
11
12
1
2
3
4
5
6
7
8

Friday

1 thing I must do:

3 actions/activities:

- ....
- ....
- ....

8
9
10
11
12
1
2
3
4
5
6
7
8

Saturday

1 thing I must do:

3 actions/activities:

- ....
- ....
- ....

8
9
10
11
12
1
2
3
4
5
6
7
8

Sunday

1 thing I must do:

3 actions/activities:

- ....
- ....
- ....

8
9
10
11
12
1
2
3
4
5
6
7
8

Social

Health

Finance

Wellbeing/Spiritual

Who Had The Most Impact?

The Best Conversation?

What Inspired You?

How Were You Brave?

What Made You Happy?

One Word Summary

What Did You Avoid?

Best Moment?

Weekly Review, week 5

On a scale of 1–10, how has this week been?

What would +1 look like?

What has worked well this week?

This week would have been even better if…

What I gave to others is:

What I received from others is:

What I appreciated:

Weekly Preview, week 6

Weekly Check-In Preview

Must do/urgent:

Must do/important:

Waiting/pending:

Delegate:

Carry forward:

1-CHECK: What's the *one* thing I *must* do this week (that will make other things easier or unnecessary):

1

3-CHECK: What are three projects/activities/actions that *must* be completed:

1

2

3

Weekly Planning, week 6

THIS WEEK'S BIG GOAL:

Monday

1 thing I must do:

3 actions/activities:

- ⬤ ....
- ⬤ ....
- ⬤ ....

8

9

10

11

12

1

2

3

4

5

6

7

8

Tuesday

1 thing I must do:

3 actions/activities:

- ⬤ ....
- ⬤ ....
- ⬤ ....

8

9

10

11

12

1

2

3

4

5

6

7

8

Wednesday

1 thing I must do:

3 actions/activities:

- ⬤ ....
- ⬤ ....
- ⬤ ....

8

9

10

11

12

1

2

3

4

5

6

7

8

WHAT HAVE YOU DONE TOWARDS ACHIEVING YOUR WHEEL OF LIFE GOALS?

Family

Business

Career

Fun

THIS WEEK'S BIG TARGET:

Thursday	Friday	Saturday	Sunday
1 thing I must do:	**1 thing I must do:**	**1 thing I must do:**	**1 thing I must do:**

3 actions/activities:

-
-
-

3 actions/activities:

-
-
-

3 actions/activities:

-
-
-

3 actions/activities:

-
-
-

Thursday	Friday	Saturday	Sunday
8	8	8	8
9	9	9	9
10	10	10	10
11	11	11	11
12	12	12	12
1	1	1	1
2	2	2	2
3	3	3	3
4	4	4	4
5	5	5	5
6	6	6	6
7	7	7	7
8	8	8	8

Social

Health

Finance

Wellbeing/Spiritual

Who Had The Most Impact?

The Best Conversation?

What Inspired You?

How Were You Brave?

What Made You Happy?

One Word Summary

What Did You Avoid?

Best Moment?

Weekly Review, week 6

On a scale of 1–10, how has this week been?

What would +1 look like?

What has worked well this week?

This week would have been even better if…

I love what I do because:

What do I need to start doing?

The elephant in the room that needs addressing is:

Weekly Preview, week 7

Weekly Check-In Preview

Must do/urgent:

Must do/important:

Waiting/pending:

Delegate:

Carry forward:

1-CHECK: What's the *one* thing I *must* do this week (that will make other things easier or unnecessary):

1

3-CHECK: What are three projects/activities/actions that *must* be completed:

1

2

3

Weekly Planning, week 7

THIS WEEK'S BIG GOAL:

Monday

1 thing I must do:

3 actions/activities:

- ....
- ....
- ....

8 ....
9 ....
10 ....
11 ....
12 ....
1 ....
2 ....
3 ....
4 ....
5 ....
6 ....
7 ....
8 ....

Tuesday

1 thing I must do:

3 actions/activities:

- ....
- ....
- ....

8 ....
9 ....
10 ....
11 ....
12 ....
1 ....
2 ....
3 ....
4 ....
5 ....
6 ....
7 ....
8 ....

Wednesday

1 thing I must do:

3 actions/activities:

- ....
- ....
- ....

8 ....
9 ....
10 ....
11 ....
12 ....
1 ....
2 ....
3 ....
4 ....
5 ....
6 ....
7 ....
8 ....

WHAT HAVE YOU DONE TOWARDS ACHIEVING YOUR WHEEL OF LIFE GOALS?

Family

Business

Career

Fun

THIS WEEK'S BIG TARGET:

Thursday

1 thing I must do:

3 actions/activities:

- ....
- ....
- ....

8 ....
9 ....
10 ....
11 ....
12 ....
1 ....
2 ....
3 ....
4 ....
5 ....
6 ....
7 ....
8 ....

Friday

1 thing I must do:

3 actions/activities:

- ....
- ....
- ....

8 ....
9 ....
10 ....
11 ....
12 ....
1 ....
2 ....
3 ....
4 ....
5 ....
6 ....
7 ....
8 ....

Saturday

1 thing I must do:

3 actions/activities:

- ....
- ....
- ....

8 ....
9 ....
10 ....
11 ....
12 ....
1 ....
2 ....
3 ....
4 ....
5 ....
6 ....
7 ....
8 ....

Sunday

1 thing I must do:

3 actions/activities:

- ....
- ....
- ....

8 ....
9 ....
10 ....
11 ....
12 ....
1 ....
2 ....
3 ....
4 ....
5 ....
6 ....
7 ....
8 ....

Social

Health

Finance

Wellbeing/Spiritual

Who Had The Most Impact?

The Best Conversation?

What Inspired You?

How Were You Brave?

What Made You Happy?

One Word Summary

What Did You Avoid?

Best Moment?

Weekly Review, week 7

On a scale of 1–10, how has this week been?

What would +1 look like?

What has worked well this week?

This week would have been even better if...

Where's the focus?

The most important upcoming meeting is:

What do I need to change and why?

Weekly Preview, week 8

Must do/urgent:

Must do/important:

Waiting/pending:

Delegate:

Carry forward:

1-CHECK: What's the *one* thing I *must* do this week (that will make other things easier or unnecessary):

1

3-CHECK: What are three projects/activities/actions that *must* be completed:

1

2

3

Weekly Planning, week 8

THIS WEEK'S BIG GOAL:

Monday

1 thing I must do:

3 actions/activities:

- ....
- ....
- ....

8 ....
9 ....
10 ....
11 ....
12 ....
1 ....
2 ....
3 ....
4 ....
5 ....
6 ....
7 ....
8 ....

Tuesday

1 thing I must do:

3 actions/activities:

- ....
- ....
- ....

8 ....
9 ....
10 ....
11 ....
12 ....
1 ....
2 ....
3 ....
4 ....
5 ....
6 ....
7 ....
8 ....

Wednesday

1 thing I must do:

3 actions/activities:

- ....
- ....
- ....

8 ....
9 ....
10 ....
11 ....
12 ....
1 ....
2 ....
3 ....
4 ....
5 ....
6 ....
7 ....
8 ....

WHAT HAVE YOU DONE TOWARDS ACHIEVING YOUR WHEEL OF LIFE GOALS?

Family

Business

Career

Fun

THIS WEEK'S BIG TARGET:

Thursday	Friday	Saturday	Sunday

1 thing I must do:

3 actions/activities:

Thursday
- ....
- ....
- ....

8
9
10
11
12
1
2
3
4
5
6
7
8

Friday
- ....
- ....
- ....

8
9
10
11
12
1
2
3
4
5
6
7
8

Saturday
- ....
- ....
- ....

8
9
10
11
12
1
2
3
4
5
6
7
8

Sunday
- ....
- ....
- ....

8
9
10
11
12
1
2
3
4
5
6
7
8

Social

Health

Finance

Wellbeing/Spiritual

Who Had The Most Impact?

The Best Conversation?

What Inspired You?

How Were You Brave?

What Made You Happy?

One Word Summary

What Did You Avoid?

Best Moment?

Weekly Review, week 8

On a scale of 1–10, how has this week been? ....

What would +1 look like? ....

What has worked well this week? ....

....

....

....

....

This week would have been even better if… ....

Who do I need to thank and why? ....

One conversation I need to have: ....

What's holding me back? ....

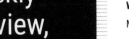

Weekly Preview, week 9

Weekly Check-In Preview

Must do/urgent:

Must do/important:

Waiting/pending:

Delegate:

Carry forward:

1-CHECK: What's the *one* thing I *must* do this week (that will make other things easier or unnecessary):

1

3-CHECK: What are three projects/activities/actions that *must* be completed:

1

2

3

Weekly Planning, week 9

Monday

1 thing I must do:

3 actions/activities:

- ....
- ....
- ....

8

9

10

11

12

1

2

3

4

5

6

7

8

Tuesday

1 thing I must do:

3 actions/activities:

- ....
- ....
- ....

8

9

10

11

12

1

2

3

4

5

6

7

8

Wednesday

1 thing I must do:

3 actions/activities:

- ....
- ....
- ....

8

9

10

11

12

1

2

3

4

5

6

7

8

WHAT HAVE YOU DONE TOWARDS ACHIEVING YOUR WHEEL OF LIFE GOALS?

Family

Business

Career

Fun

THIS WEEK'S BIG TARGET:

Thursday

1 thing I must do:

3 actions/activities:

- ....
- ....
- ....

8 ....
9 ....
10 ....
11 ....
12 ....
1 ....
2 ....
3 ....
4 ....
5 ....
6 ....
7 ....
8 ....

Friday

1 thing I must do:

3 actions/activities:

- ....
- ....
- ....

8 ....
9 ....
10 ....
11 ....
12 ....
1 ....
2 ....
3 ....
4 ....
5 ....
6 ....
7 ....
8 ....

Saturday

1 thing I must do:

3 actions/activities:

- ....
- ....
- ....

8 ....
9 ....
10 ....
11 ....
12 ....
1 ....
2 ....
3 ....
4 ....
5 ....
6 ....
7 ....
8 ....

Sunday

1 thing I must do:

3 actions/activities:

- ....
- ....
- ....

8 ....
9 ....
10 ....
11 ....
12 ....
1 ....
2 ....
3 ....
4 ....
5 ....
6 ....
7 ....
8 ....

Social

Health

Finance

Wellbeing/Spiritual

Who Had The Most Impact?

The Best Conversation?

What Inspired You?

How Were You Brave?

What Made You Happy?

One Word Summary

What Did You Avoid?

Best Moment?

Weekly Review, week 9

On a scale of 1–10, how has this week been?

What would +1 look like?

What has worked well this week?

This week would have been even better if...

What I gave to others is:

What I received from others is:

What I appreciated:

Weekly Preview, week 10

Weekly Check-In Preview

Must do/urgent:

Must do/important:

Waiting/pending:

Delegate:

Carry forward:

1-CHECK: What's the *one* thing I *must* do this week (that will make other things easier or unnecessary):

1

3-CHECK: What are three projects/activities/actions that *must* be completed:

1

2

3

Weekly Planning, week 10

THIS WEEK'S BIG GOAL:

Monday

1 thing I must do:

3 actions/activities:

- ....
- ....
- ....

8 ....
9 ....
10 ....
11 ....
12 ....
1 ....
2 ....
3 ....
4 ....
5 ....
6 ....
7 ....
8 ....

Tuesday

1 thing I must do:

3 actions/activities:

- ....
- ....
- ....

8 ....
9 ....
10 ....
11 ....
12 ....
1 ....
2 ....
3 ....
4 ....
5 ....
6 ....
7 ....
8 ....

Wednesday

1 thing I must do:

3 actions/activities:

- ....
- ....
- ....

8 ....
9 ....
10 ....
11 ....
12 ....
1 ....
2 ....
3 ....
4 ....
5 ....
6 ....
7 ....
8 ....

WHAT HAVE YOU DONE TOWARDS ACHIEVING YOUR WHEEL OF LIFE GOALS?

Family

Business

Career

Fun

THIS WEEK'S BIG TARGET:

Thursday

1 thing I must do:

3 actions/activities:

- ....
- ....
- ....

8
9
10
11
12
1
2
3
4
5
6
7
8

Friday

1 thing I must do:

3 actions/activities:

- ....
- ....
- ....

8
9
10
11
12
1
2
3
4
5
6
7
8

Saturday

1 thing I must do:

3 actions/activities:

- ....
- ....
- ....

8
9
10
11
12
1
2
3
4
5
6
7
8

Sunday

1 thing I must do:

3 actions/activities:

- ....
- ....
- ....

8
9
10
11
12
1
2
3
4
5
6
7
8

Social

Health

Finance

Wellbeing/Spiritual

Who Had The Most Impact?

The Best Conversation?

What Inspired You?

How Were You Brave?

What Made You Happy?

One Word Summary

What Did You Avoid?

Best Moment?

Weekly Review, week 10

On a scale of 1–10, how has this week been?

What would +1 look like?

What has worked well this week?

This week would have been even better if…

I love what I do because:

What do I need to start doing?

The elephant in the room that needs addressing is:

Weekly Preview, week 11

Weekly Check-In Preview

Must do/urgent:

Must do/important:

Waiting/pending:

Delegate:

Carry forward:

1-CHECK: What's the *one* thing I *must* do this week (that will make other things easier or unnecessary):

1

3-CHECK: What are three projects/activities/actions that *must* be completed:

1

2

3

Weekly Planning, week 11

THIS WEEK'S BIG GOAL:

Monday

1 thing I must do:

3 actions/activities:

-
-
-

8

9

10

11

12

1

2

3

4

5

6

7

8

Tuesday

1 thing I must do:

3 actions/activities:

-
-
-

8

9

10

11

12

1

2

3

4

5

6

7

8

Wednesday

1 thing I must do:

3 actions/activities:

-
-
-

8

9

10

11

12

1

2

3

4

5

6

7

8

WHAT HAVE YOU DONE TOWARDS ACHIEVING YOUR WHEEL OF LIFE GOALS?

Family

Business

Career

Fun

THIS WEEK'S BIG TARGET:

Thursday	Friday	Saturday	Sunday

1 thing I must do:

3 actions/activities:

- •
- •
- •

Thursday	Friday	Saturday	Sunday
8	8	8	8
9	9	9	9
10	10	10	10
11	11	11	11
12	12	12	12
1	1	1	1
2	2	2	2
3	3	3	3
4	4	4	4
5	5	5	5
6	6	6	6
7	7	7	7
8	8	8	8

Social

Health

Finance

Wellbeing/Spiritual

Who Had The Most Impact?

The Best Conversation?

What Inspired You?

How Were You Brave?

What Made You Happy?

One Word Summary

What Did You Avoid?

Best Moment?

Weekly Review, week 11

On a scale of 1–10, how has this week been? ....

What would +1 look like? ....

What has worked well this week? ....

....

....

....

This week would have been even better if... ....

Where's the focus? ....

The most important upcoming meeting is: ....

What do I need to change and why? ....

Weekly Preview, week 12

Weekly Check-In Preview

Must do/urgent:

Must do/important:

Waiting/pending:

Delegate:

Carry forward:

1-CHECK: What's the *one* thing I *must* do this week (that will make other things easier or unnecessary):

1

3-CHECK: What are three projects/activities/actions that *must* be completed:

1

2

3

Weekly Planning, week 12

THIS WEEK'S BIG GOAL:

Monday

1 thing I must do:

3 actions/activities:

-
-
-

8
9
10
11
12
1
2
3
4
5
6
7
8

Tuesday

1 thing I must do:

3 actions/activities:

-
-
-

8
9
10
11
12
1
2
3
4
5
6
7
8

Wednesday

1 thing I must do:

3 actions/activities:

-
-
-

8
9
10
11
12
1
2
3
4
5
6
7
8

WHAT HAVE YOU DONE TOWARDS ACHIEVING YOUR WHEEL OF LIFE GOALS?

Family

Business

Career

Fun

THIS WEEK'S BIG TARGET:

Thursday

1 thing I must do:

3 actions/activities:

- ....
- ....
- ....

8 ....
9 ....
10 ....
11 ....
12 ....
1 ....
2 ....
3 ....
4 ....
5 ....
6 ....
7 ....
8 ....

Friday

1 thing I must do:

3 actions/activities:

- ....
- ....
- ....

8 ....
9 ....
10 ....
11 ....
12 ....
1 ....
2 ....
3 ....
4 ....
5 ....
6 ....
7 ....
8 ....

Saturday

1 thing I must do:

3 actions/activities:

- ....
- ....
- ....

8 ....
9 ....
10 ....
11 ....
12 ....
1 ....
2 ....
3 ....
4 ....
5 ....
6 ....
7 ....
8 ....

Sunday

1 thing I must do:

3 actions/activities:

- ....
- ....
- ....

8 ....
9 ....
10 ....
11 ....
12 ....
1 ....
2 ....
3 ....
4 ....
5 ....
6 ....
7 ....
8 ....

Social

Health

Finance

Wellbeing/Spiritual

Who Had The Most Impact?

The Best Conversation?

What Inspired You?

How Were You Brave?

What Made You Happy?

One Word Summary

What Did You Avoid?

Best Moment?

Weekly Review, week 12

On a scale of 1–10, how has this week been?

What would +1 look like?

What has worked well this week?

This week would have been even better if…

Who do I need to thank and why?

One conversation I need to have:

What's holding me back?

Weekly Preview, week 13

Weekly Check-In Preview

Must do/urgent:

Must do/important:

Waiting/pending:

Delegate:

Carry forward:

1-CHECK: What's the *one* thing I *must* do this week (that will make other things easier or unnecessary):

1

3-CHECK: What are three projects/activities/actions that *must* be completed:

1

2

3

Weekly Planning, week 13

THIS WEEK'S BIG GOAL:

Monday

1 thing I must do:

3 actions/activities:

- ....
- ....
- ....

8

9

10

11

12

1

2

3

4

5

6

7

8

Tuesday

1 thing I must do:

3 actions/activities:

- ....
- ....
- ....

8

9

10

11

12

1

2

3

4

5

6

7

8

Wednesday

1 thing I must do:

3 actions/activities:

- ....
- ....
- ....

8

9

10

11

12

1

2

3

4

5

6

7

8

WHAT HAVE YOU DONE TOWARDS ACHIEVING YOUR WHEEL OF LIFE GOALS?

Family

Business

Career

Fun

THIS WEEK'S BIG TARGET:

Thursday

1 thing I must do:

3 actions/activities:

- ....
- ....
- ....

8
9
10
11
12
1
2
3
4
5
6
7
8

Friday

1 thing I must do:

3 actions/activities:

- ....
- ....
- ....

8
9
10
11
12
1
2
3
4
5
6
7
8

Saturday

1 thing I must do:

3 actions/activities:

- ....
- ....
- ....

8
9
10
11
12
1
2
3
4
5
6
7
8

Sunday

1 thing I must do:

3 actions/activities:

- ....
- ....
- ....

8
9
10
11
12
1
2
3
4
5
6
7
8

Social	Who Had The Most Impact?	What Made You Happy?
Health	The Best Conversation?	One Word Summary
Finance	What Inspired You?	What Did You Avoid?
Wellbeing/Spiritual	How Were You Brave?	Best Moment?

Weekly Review, week 13

On a scale of 1–10, how has this week been?

What would +1 look like?

What has worked well this week?

This week would have been even better if...

As we approach the end of the quarter, what have you failed to do?

What do you need to check?

Who do you still need to contact?

Q2 Quarterly Review

What do you feel were your most significant accomplishments?

Professional/Business:

Personal/Family:

What do you feel were your most significant disappointments?

Professional/Business:

Personal/Family:

Q2 Quarterly Business Review

AREA/INITIATIVE	SCORE OUT OF 10	WHY
FINANCIAL:		
MARKETING:		
OPERATIONS:		
PEOPLE & CULTURE:		
OTHER:		

Q2
Quarterly
Personal
Review

AREA/INITIATIVE	SCORE OUT OF 10	WHY
FAMILY		
BUSINESS		
CAREER		
FUN		
SOCIAL		
HEALTH		
FINANCE		
WELLBEING/SPIRITUAL		

NOTES

NOTES

NOTES

Q3
Quarterly
Business
Plan

Instructions: This quarterly plan should be created by looking at the annual plan on page 35 and applying the relevant data to this quarter.

AREA/INITIATIVE	BUDGET	WHO	WHEN
FINANCIAL:			
MARKETING:			
OPERATIONS:			
PEOPLE:			
OTHER:			

Q3 Quarterly Personal Plan

Instructions: This quarterly plan should be created by looking at the annual personal plan on page 42 and applying the relevant data to this quarter.

AREA/INITIATIVE	OUTCOME	WHEN
FAMILY		
BUSINESS		
CAREER		
FUN		
SOCIAL		
HEALTH		
FINANCE		
WELLBEING/SPIRITUAL		

Weekly Preview, week 1

Weekly Check-In Preview

Must do/urgent:

Must do/important:

Waiting/pending:

Delegate:

Carry forward:

1-CHECK: What's the *one* thing I *must* do this week (that will make other things easier or unnecessary):

1

3-CHECK: What are three projects/activities/actions that *must* be completed:

1

2

3

Weekly Planning, week 1

THIS WEEK'S BIG GOAL:

Monday	Tuesday	Wednesday
1 thing I must do:	**1 thing I must do:**	**1 thing I must do:**
3 actions/activities:	3 actions/activities:	3 actions/activities:

Monday
-
-
-

8
9
10
11
12
1
2
3
4
5
6
7
8

Tuesday
-
-
-

8
9
10
11
12
1
2
3
4
5
6
7
8

Wednesday
-
-
-

8
9
10
11
12
1
2
3
4
5
6
7
8

WHAT HAVE YOU DONE TOWARDS ACHIEVING YOUR WHEEL OF LIFE GOALS?

Family

Business

Career

Fun

THIS WEEK'S BIG TARGET:

Thursday

1 thing I must do:

3 actions/activities:

- ....
- ....
- ....

8 ....
9 ....
10 ....
11 ....
12 ....
1 ....
2 ....
3 ....
4 ....
5 ....
6 ....
7 ....
8 ....

Friday

1 thing I must do:

3 actions/activities:

- ....
- ....
- ....

8 ....
9 ....
10 ....
11 ....
12 ....
1 ....
2 ....
3 ....
4 ....
5 ....
6 ....
7 ....
8 ....

Saturday

1 thing I must do:

3 actions/activities:

- ....
- ....
- ....

8 ....
9 ....
10 ....
11 ....
12 ....
1 ....
2 ....
3 ....
4 ....
5 ....
6 ....
7 ....
8 ....

Sunday

1 thing I must do:

3 actions/activities:

- ....
- ....
- ....

8 ....
9 ....
10 ....
11 ....
12 ....
1 ....
2 ....
3 ....
4 ....
5 ....
6 ....
7 ....
8 ....

Social

Health

Finance

Wellbeing/Spiritual

Who Had The Most Impact?

The Best Conversation?

What Inspired You?

How Were You Brave?

What Made You Happy?

One Word Summary

What Did You Avoid?

Best Moment?

Weekly Review, week 1

On a scale of 1–10, how has this week been? ....

What would +1 look like? ....

What has worked well this week? ....

....

....

....

....

This week would have been even better if... ....

What I gave to others is: ....

What I received from others is: ....

What I appreciated: ....

Weekly Preview, week 2

Weekly Check-In Preview

Must do/urgent:

Must do/important:

Waiting/pending:

Delegate:

Carry forward:

1-CHECK: What's the *one* thing I *must* do this week (that will make other things easier or unnecessary):

1

3-CHECK: What are three projects/activities/actions that *must* be completed:

1

2

3

Weekly Planning, week 2

THIS WEEK'S BIG GOAL:

Monday

1 thing I must do:

3 actions/activities:

- ....
- ....
- ....

8
9
10
11
12
1
2
3
4
5
6
7
8

Tuesday

1 thing I must do:

3 actions/activities:

- ....
- ....
- ....

8
9
10
11
12
1
2
3
4
5
6
7
8

Wednesday

1 thing I must do:

3 actions/activities:

- ....
- ....
- ....

8
9
10
11
12
1
2
3
4
5
6
7
8

WHAT HAVE YOU DONE TOWARDS ACHIEVING YOUR WHEEL OF LIFE GOALS?

Family

Business

Career

Fun

THIS WEEK'S BIG TARGET:

Thursday

1 thing I must do:

3 actions/activities:

-
-
-

8

9

10

11

12

1

2

3

4

5

6

7

8

Friday

1 thing I must do:

3 actions/activities:

-
-
-

8

9

10

11

12

1

2

3

4

5

6

7

8

Saturday

1 thing I must do:

3 actions/activities:

-
-
-

8

9

10

11

12

1

2

3

4

5

6

7

8

Sunday

1 thing I must do:

3 actions/activities:

-
-
-

8

9

10

11

12

1

2

3

4

5

6

7

8

Social

Health

Finance

Wellbeing/Spiritual

Who Had The Most Impact?

The Best Conversation?

What Inspired You?

How Were You Brave?

What Made You Happy?

One Word Summary

What Did You Avoid?

Best Moment?

Weekly Review, week 2

On a scale of 1–10, how has this week been?

What would +1 look like?

What has worked well this week?

This week would have been even better if…

I love what I do because:

What do I need to start doing?

The elephant in the room that needs addressing is:

Weekly Preview, week 3

Weekly Check-In Preview

Must do/urgent:

Must do/important:

Waiting/pending:

Delegate:

Carry forward:

1-CHECK: What's the *one* thing I *must* do this week (that will make other things easier or unnecessary):

1

3-CHECK: What are three projects/activities/actions that *must* be completed:

1

2

3

Weekly Planning, week 3

THIS WEEK'S BIG GOAL:

Monday

1 thing I must do:

3 actions/activities:

- ....
- ....
- ....

8
9
10
11
12
1
2
3
4
5
6
7
8

Tuesday

1 thing I must do:

3 actions/activities:

- ....
- ....
- ....

8
9
10
11
12
1
2
3
4
5
6
7
8

Wednesday

1 thing I must do:

3 actions/activities:

- ....
- ....
- ....

8
9
10
11
12
1
2
3
4
5
6
7
8

WHAT HAVE YOU DONE TOWARDS ACHIEVING YOUR WHEEL OF LIFE GOALS?

Family

Business

Career

Fun

THIS WEEK'S BIG TARGET:

Thursday

1 thing I must do:

3 actions/activities:

- _____
- _____
- _____

8

9

10

11

12

1

2

3

4

5

6

7

8

Friday

1 thing I must do:

3 actions/activities:

- _____
- _____
- _____

8

9

10

11

12

1

2

3

4

5

6

7

8

Saturday

1 thing I must do:

3 actions/activities:

- _____
- _____
- _____

8

9

10

11

12

1

2

3

4

5

6

7

8

Sunday

1 thing I must do:

3 actions/activities:

- _____
- _____
- _____

8

9

10

11

12

1

2

3

4

5

6

7

8

Social

Health

Finance

Wellbeing/Spiritual

Who Had The Most Impact?

The Best Conversation?

What Inspired You?

How Were You Brave?

What Made You Happy?

One Word Summary

What Did You Avoid?

Best Moment?

Weekly Review, week 3

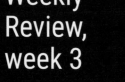

On a scale of 1–10, how has this week been?

What would +1 look like?

What has worked well this week?

This week would have been even better if...

Where's the focus?

The most important upcoming meeting is:

What do I need to change and why?

Weekly Preview, week 4

Weekly Check-In Preview

Must do/urgent:

Must do/important:

Waiting/pending:

Delegate:

Carry forward:

1-CHECK: What's the *one* thing I *must* do this week (that will make other things easier or unnecessary):

1

3-CHECK: What are three projects/activities/actions that *must* be completed:

1

2

3

Weekly Planning, week 4

Monday

1 thing I must do:

3 actions/activities:

- ....
- ....
- ....

8
9
10
11
12
1
2
3
4
5
6
7
8

Tuesday

1 thing I must do:

3 actions/activities:

- ....
- ....
- ....

8
9
10
11
12
1
2
3
4
5
6
7
8

Wednesday

1 thing I must do:

3 actions/activities:

- ....
- ....
- ....

8
9
10
11
12
1
2
3
4
5
6
7
8

WHAT HAVE YOU DONE TOWARDS ACHIEVING YOUR WHEEL OF LIFE GOALS?

Family

Business

Career

Fun

THIS WEEK'S BIG TARGET:

Thursday	Friday	Saturday	Sunday

1 thing I must do:

3 actions/activities:

- ·································
- ·································
- ·································

8
9
10
11
12
1
2
3
4
5
6
7
8

1 thing I must do:

3 actions/activities:

- ·································
- ·································
- ·································

8
9
10
11
12
1
2
3
4
5
6
7
8

1 thing I must do:

3 actions/activities:

- ·································
- ·································
- ·································

8
9
10
11
12
1
2
3
4
5
6
7
8

1 thing I must do:

3 actions/activities:

- ·································
- ·································
- ·································

8
9
10
11
12
1
2
3
4
5
6
7
8

Social

Health

Finance

Wellbeing/Spiritual

Who Had The Most Impact?

The Best Conversation?

What Inspired You?

How Were You Brave?

What Made You Happy?

One Word Summary

What Did You Avoid?

Best Moment?

Weekly Review, week 4

On a scale of 1–10, how has this week been?

What would +1 look like?

What has worked well this week?

This week would have been even better if...

Who do I need to thank and why?

One conversation I need to have:

What's holding me back?

Weekly Preview, week 5

Weekly Check-In Preview

Must do/urgent:

Must do/important:

Waiting/pending:

Delegate:

Carry forward:

1-CHECK: What's the *one* thing I *must* do this week (that will make other things easier or unnecessary):

1

3-CHECK: What are three projects/activities/actions that *must* be completed:

1

2

3

Weekly Planning, week 5

THIS WEEK'S BIG GOAL:

Monday

1 thing I must do:

3 actions/activities:

- ·································
- ·································
- ·································

8
9
10
11
12
1
2
3
4
5
6
7
8

Tuesday

1 thing I must do:

3 actions/activities:

- ·································
- ·································
- ·································

8
9
10
11
12
1
2
3
4
5
6
7
8

Wednesday

1 thing I must do:

3 actions/activities:

- ·································
- ·································
- ·································

8
9
10
11
12
1
2
3
4
5
6
7
8

**WHAT HAVE YOU DONE TOWARDS ACHIEVING
YOUR WHEEL OF LIFE GOALS?**

Family

Business

Career

Fun

THIS WEEK'S BIG TARGET:

Thursday	Friday	Saturday	Sunday

1 thing I must do: **1 thing I must do:**   **1 thing I must do:**   **1 thing I must do:**

3 actions/activities: 3 actions/activities: 3 actions/activities: 3 actions/activities:

-
-
-

8

9

10

11

12

1

2

3

4

5

6

7

8

Social

Health

Finance

Wellbeing/Spiritual

Who Had The Most Impact?

The Best Conversation?

What Inspired You?

How Were You Brave?

What Made You Happy?

One Word Summary

What Did You Avoid?

Best Moment?

Weekly Review, week 5

On a scale of 1–10, how has this week been?

What would +1 look like?

What has worked well this week?

This week would have been even better if...

What I gave to others is:

What I received from others is:

What I appreciated:

Weekly Preview, week 6

Weekly Check-In Preview

Must do/urgent:

Must do/important:

Waiting/pending:

Delegate:

Carry forward:

1-CHECK: What's the *one* thing I *must* do this week (that will make other things easier or unnecessary):

1

3-CHECK: What are three projects/activities/actions that *must* be completed:

1

2

3

Weekly Planning, week 6

THIS WEEK'S BIG GOAL:

Monday

1 thing I must do:

3 actions/activities:

- ....
- ....
- ....

8 ....
9 ....
10 ....
11 ....
12 ....
1 ....
2 ....
3 ....
4 ....
5 ....
6 ....
7 ....
8 ....

Tuesday

1 thing I must do:

3 actions/activities:

- ....
- ....
- ....

8 ....
9 ....
10 ....
11 ....
12 ....
1 ....
2 ....
3 ....
4 ....
5 ....
6 ....
7 ....
8 ....

Wednesday

1 thing I must do:

3 actions/activities:

- ....
- ....
- ....

8 ....
9 ....
10 ....
11 ....
12 ....
1 ....
2 ....
3 ....
4 ....
5 ....
6 ....
7 ....
8 ....

WHAT HAVE YOU DONE TOWARDS ACHIEVING YOUR WHEEL OF LIFE GOALS?

Family

Business

Career

Fun

THIS WEEK'S BIG TARGET:

Thursday	Friday	Saturday	Sunday
1 thing I must do:	**1 thing I must do:**	**1 thing I must do:**	**1 thing I must do:**
3 actions/activities:	3 actions/activities:	3 actions/activities:	3 actions/activities:

Thursday

1 thing I must do:

3 actions/activities:

-
-
-

8
9
10
11
12
1
2
3
4
5
6
7
8

Friday

1 thing I must do:

3 actions/activities:

-
-
-

8
9
10
11
12
1
2
3
4
5
6
7
8

Saturday

1 thing I must do:

3 actions/activities:

-
-
-

8
9
10
11
12
1
2
3
4
5
6
7
8

Sunday

1 thing I must do:

3 actions/activities:

-
-
-

8
9
10
11
12
1
2
3
4
5
6
7
8

Social

Health

Finance

Wellbeing/Spiritual

Who Had The Most Impact?

The Best Conversation?

What Inspired You?

How Were You Brave?

What Made You Happy?

One Word Summary

What Did You Avoid?

Best Moment?

Weekly Review, week 6

On a scale of 1–10, how has this week been? ....

What would +1 look like? ....

What has worked well this week? ....

....

....

....

This week would have been even better if... ....

I love what I do because: ....

What do I need to start doing? ....

The elephant in the room that needs addressing is: ....

Weekly Preview, week 7

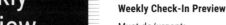

Weekly Check-In Preview

Must do/urgent:

Must do/important:

Waiting/pending:

Delegate:

Carry forward:

1-CHECK: What's the *one* thing I *must* do this week (that will make other things easier or unnecessary):

1

3-CHECK: What are three projects/activities/actions that *must* be completed:

1

2

3

Weekly Planning, week 7

THIS WEEK'S BIG GOAL:

Monday

1 thing I must do:

3 actions/activities:

- ....
- ....
- ....

8
9
10
11
12
1
2
3
4
5
6
7
8

Tuesday

1 thing I must do:

3 actions/activities:

- ....
- ....
- ....

8
9
10
11
12
1
2
3
4
5
6
7
8

Wednesday

1 thing I must do:

3 actions/activities:

- ....
- ....
- ....

8
9
10
11
12
1
2
3
4
5
6
7
8

WHAT HAVE YOU DONE TOWARDS ACHIEVING YOUR WHEEL OF LIFE GOALS?

Family

Business

Career

Fun

THIS WEEK'S BIG TARGET:

Thursday	Friday	Saturday	Sunday

1 thing I must do:

3 actions/activities:

Thursday

1 thing I must do:

3 actions/activities:

-
-
-

8

9

10

11

12

1

2

3

4

5

6

7

8

Friday

1 thing I must do:

3 actions/activities:

-
-
-

8

9

10

11

12

1

2

3

4

5

6

7

8

Saturday

1 thing I must do:

3 actions/activities:

-
-
-

8

9

10

11

12

1

2

3

4

5

6

7

8

Sunday

1 thing I must do:

3 actions/activities:

-
-
-

8

9

10

11

12

1

2

3

4

5

6

7

8

Social

Health

Finance

Wellbeing/Spiritual

Who Had The Most Impact?

The Best Conversation?

What Inspired You?

How Were You Brave?

What Made You Happy?

One Word Summary

What Did You Avoid?

Best Moment?

Weekly Review, week 7

On a scale of 1–10, how has this week been?

What would +1 look like?

What has worked well this week?

This week would have been even better if...

Where's the focus?

The most important upcoming meeting is:

What do I need to change and why?

Weekly Preview, week 8

Weekly Check-In Preview

Must do/urgent:

Must do/important:

Waiting/pending:

Delegate:

Carry forward:

1-CHECK: What's the *one* thing I *must* do this week (that will make other things easier or unnecessary):

1

3-CHECK: What are three projects/activities/actions that *must* be completed:

1

2

3

Weekly Planning, week 8

THIS WEEK'S BIG GOAL:

Monday

1 thing I must do:

3 actions/activities:

-
-
-

8
9
10
11
12
1
2
3
4
5
6
7
8

Tuesday

1 thing I must do:

3 actions/activities:

-
-
-

8
9
10
11
12
1
2
3
4
5
6
7
8

Wednesday

1 thing I must do:

3 actions/activities:

-
-
-

8
9
10
11
12
1
2
3
4
5
6
7
8

WHAT HAVE YOU DONE TOWARDS ACHIEVING YOUR WHEEL OF LIFE GOALS?

Family

Business

Career

Fun

THIS WEEK'S BIG TARGET:

Thursday	Friday	Saturday	Sunday

1 thing I must do:

3 actions/activities:

Thursday

1 thing I must do:

3 actions/activities:

- _____
- _____
- _____

8
9
10
11
12
1
2
3
4
5
6
7
8

Friday

1 thing I must do:

3 actions/activities:

- _____
- _____
- _____

8
9
10
11
12
1
2
3
4
5
6
7
8

Saturday

1 thing I must do:

3 actions/activities:

- _____
- _____
- _____

8
9
10
11
12
1
2
3
4
5
6
7
8

Sunday

1 thing I must do:

3 actions/activities:

- _____
- _____
- _____

8
9
10
11
12
1
2
3
4
5
6
7
8

Social

Health

Finance

Wellbeing/Spiritual

Who Had The Most Impact?

The Best Conversation?

What Inspired You?

How Were You Brave?

What Made You Happy?

One Word Summary

What Did You Avoid?

Best Moment?

Weekly Review, week 8

On a scale of 1–10, how has this week been?

What would +1 look like?

What has worked well this week?

This week would have been even better if…

Who do I need to thank and why?

One conversation I need to have:

What's holding me back?

Weekly Preview, week 9

Weekly Check-In Preview

Must do/urgent:

Must do/important:

Waiting/pending:

Delegate:

Carry forward:

1-CHECK: What's the *one* thing I *must* do this week (that will make other things easier or unnecessary):

1

3-CHECK: What are three projects/activities/actions that *must* be completed:

1

2

3

Weekly Planning, week 9

THIS WEEK'S BIG GOAL:

Monday

1 thing I must do:

3 actions/activities:

- ....
- ....
- ....

8
9
10
11
12
1
2
3
4
5
6
7
8

Tuesday

1 thing I must do:

3 actions/activities:

- ....
- ....
- ....

8
9
10
11
12
1
2
3
4
5
6
7
8

Wednesday

1 thing I must do:

3 actions/activities:

- ....
- ....
- ....

8
9
10
11
12
1
2
3
4
5
6
7
8

WHAT HAVE YOU DONE TOWARDS ACHIEVING YOUR WHEEL OF LIFE GOALS?

Family

Business

Career

Fun

THIS WEEK'S BIG TARGET:

Thursday

1 thing I must do:

3 actions/activities:

-
-
-

8

9

10

11

12

1

2

3

4

5

6

7

8

Friday

1 thing I must do:

3 actions/activities:

-
-
-

8

9

10

11

12

1

2

3

4

5

6

7

8

Saturday

1 thing I must do:

3 actions/activities:

-
-
-

8

9

10

11

12

1

2

3

4

5

6

7

8

Sunday

1 thing I must do:

3 actions/activities:

-
-
-

8

9

10

11

12

1

2

3

4

5

6

7

8

Social

Health

Finance

Wellbeing/Spiritual

Who Had The Most Impact?

The Best Conversation?

What Inspired You?

How Were You Brave?

What Made You Happy?

One Word Summary

What Did You Avoid?

Best Moment?

Weekly Review, week 9

On a scale of 1–10, how has this week been? ....

What would +1 look like? ....

What has worked well this week? ....

....

....

....

This week would have been even better if... ....

What I gave to others is: ....

What I received from others is: ....

What I appreciated: ....

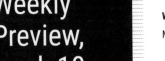

Weekly Preview, week 10

Weekly Check-In Preview

Must do/urgent:

Must do/important:

Waiting/pending:

Delegate:

Carry forward:

1-CHECK: What's the *one* thing I *must* do this week (that will make other things easier or unnecessary):

1

3-CHECK: What are three projects/activities/actions that *must* be completed:

1

2

3

Weekly Planning, week 10

THIS WEEK'S BIG GOAL:

Monday

1 thing I must do:

3 actions/activities:

-
-
-

8

9

10

11

12

1

2

3

4

5

6

7

8

Tuesday

1 thing I must do:

3 actions/activities:

-
-
-

8

9

10

11

12

1

2

3

4

5

6

7

8

Wednesday

1 thing I must do:

3 actions/activities:

-
-
-

8

9

10

11

12

1

2

3

4

5

6

7

8

WHAT HAVE YOU DONE TOWARDS ACHIEVING YOUR WHEEL OF LIFE GOALS?

Family

Business

Career

Fun

THIS WEEK'S BIG TARGET:

Thursday

1 thing I must do:

3 actions/activities:

- ....
- ....
- ....

8 ....
9 ....
10 ....
11 ....
12 ....
1 ....
2 ....
3 ....
4 ....
5 ....
6 ....
7 ....
8 ....

Friday

1 thing I must do:

3 actions/activities:

- ....
- ....
- ....

8 ....
9 ....
10 ....
11 ....
12 ....
1 ....
2 ....
3 ....
4 ....
5 ....
6 ....
7 ....
8 ....

Saturday

1 thing I must do:

3 actions/activities:

- ....
- ....
- ....

8 ....
9 ....
10 ....
11 ....
12 ....
1 ....
2 ....
3 ....
4 ....
5 ....
6 ....
7 ....
8 ....

Sunday

1 thing I must do:

3 actions/activities:

- ....
- ....
- ....

8 ....
9 ....
10 ....
11 ....
12 ....
1 ....
2 ....
3 ....
4 ....
5 ....
6 ....
7 ....
8 ....

Social

Health

Finance

Wellbeing/Spiritual

Who Had The Most Impact?

The Best Conversation?

What Inspired You?

How Were You Brave?

What Made You Happy?

One Word Summary

What Did You Avoid?

Best Moment?

205

Weekly Review, week 10

On a scale of 1–10, how has this week been? ....

What would +1 look like? ....

What has worked well this week? ....

....

....

....

....

....

This week would have been even better if… ....

I love what I do because: ....

What do I need to start doing? ....

The elephant in the room that needs addressing is: ....

Weekly Preview, week 11

Weekly Check-In Preview

Must do/urgent:

Must do/important:

Waiting/pending:

Delegate:

Carry forward:

1-CHECK: What's the *one* thing I *must* do this week (that will make other things easier or unnecessary):

1

3-CHECK: What are three projects/activities/actions that *must* be completed:

1

2

3

Weekly Planning, week 11

THIS WEEK'S BIG GOAL:

Monday

1 thing I must do:

3 actions/activities:

- ....
- ....
- ....

8
9
10
11
12
1
2
3
4
5
6
7
8

Tuesday

1 thing I must do:

3 actions/activities:

- ....
- ....
- ....

8
9
10
11
12
1
2
3
4
5
6
7
8

Wednesday

1 thing I must do:

3 actions/activities:

- ....
- ....
- ....

8
9
10
11
12
1
2
3
4
5
6
7
8

WHAT HAVE YOU DONE TOWARDS ACHIEVING YOUR WHEEL OF LIFE GOALS?

Family

Business

Career

Fun

THIS WEEK'S BIG TARGET:

Thursday

1 thing I must do:

3 actions/activities:

- ....
- ....
- ....

8
9
10
11
12
1
2
3
4
5
6
7
8

Friday

1 thing I must do:

3 actions/activities:

- ....
- ....
- ....

8
9
10
11
12
1
2
3
4
5
6
7
8

Saturday

1 thing I must do:

3 actions/activities:

- ....
- ....
- ....

8
9
10
11
12
1
2
3
4
5
6
7
8

Sunday

1 thing I must do:

3 actions/activities:

- ....
- ....
- ....

8
9
10
11
12
1
2
3
4
5
6
7
8

Social

Health

Finance

Wellbeing/Spiritual

Who Had The Most Impact?

The Best Conversation?

What Inspired You?

How Were You Brave?

What Made You Happy?

One Word Summary

What Did You Avoid?

Best Moment?

Weekly Review, week 11

On a scale of 1–10, how has this week been?

What would +1 look like?

What has worked well this week?

This week would have been even better if...

Where's the focus?

The most important upcoming meeting is:

What do I need to change and why?

Weekly Preview, week 12

Weekly Check-In Preview

Must do/urgent:

Must do/important:

Waiting/pending:

Delegate:

Carry forward:

1-CHECK: What's the *one* thing I *must* do this week (that will make other things easier or unnecessary):

1

3-CHECK: What are three projects/activities/actions that *must* be completed:

1

2

3

Weekly Planning, week 12

THIS WEEK'S BIG GOAL:

Monday

1 thing I must do:

3 actions/activities:

- ....
- ....
- ....

8

9

10

11

12

1

2

3

4

5

6

7

8

Tuesday

1 thing I must do:

3 actions/activities:

- ....
- ....
- ....

8

9

10

11

12

1

2

3

4

5

6

7

8

Wednesday

1 thing I must do:

3 actions/activities:

- ....
- ....
- ....

8

9

10

11

12

1

2

3

4

5

6

7

8

WHAT HAVE YOU DONE TOWARDS ACHIEVING YOUR WHEEL OF LIFE GOALS?

Family

Business

Career

Fun

THIS WEEK'S BIG TARGET:

Thursday

1 thing I must do:

3 actions/activities:

- ⬤ ....
- ⬤ ....
- ⬤ ....

8
9
10
11
12
1
2
3
4
5
6
7
8

Friday

1 thing I must do:

3 actions/activities:

- ⬤ ....
- ⬤ ....
- ⬤ ....

8
9
10
11
12
1
2
3
4
5
6
7
8

Saturday

1 thing I must do:

3 actions/activities:

- ⬤ ....
- ⬤ ....
- ⬤ ....

8
9
10
11
12
1
2
3
4
5
6
7
8

Sunday

1 thing I must do:

3 actions/activities:

- ⬤ ....
- ⬤ ....
- ⬤ ....

8
9
10
11
12
1
2
3
4
5
6
7
8

Social

Health

Finance

Wellbeing/Spiritual

Who Had The Most Impact?

The Best Conversation?

What Inspired You?

How Were You Brave?

What Made You Happy?

One Word Summary

What Did You Avoid?

Best Moment?

Weekly Review, week 12

On a scale of 1–10, how has this week been?

What would +1 look like?

What has worked well this week?

This week would have been even better if…

Who do I need to thank and why?

One conversation I need to have:

What's holding me back?

Weekly Preview, week 13

Weekly Check-In Preview

Must do/urgent:

Must do/important:

Waiting/pending:

Delegate:

Carry forward:

1-CHECK: What's the *one* thing I *must* do this week (that will make other things easier or unnecessary):

1

3-CHECK: What are three projects/activities/actions that *must* be completed:

1

2

3

Weekly Planning, week 13

Monday

1 thing I must do:

3 actions/activities:

- ....
- ....
- ....

8 ....

9 ....

10 ....

11 ....

12 ....

1 ....

2 ....

3 ....

4 ....

5 ....

6 ....

7 ....

8 ....

Tuesday

1 thing I must do:

3 actions/activities:

- ....
- ....
- ....

8 ....

9 ....

10 ....

11 ....

12 ....

1 ....

2 ....

3 ....

4 ....

5 ....

6 ....

7 ....

8 ....

Wednesday

1 thing I must do:

3 actions/activities:

- ....
- ....
- ....

8 ....

9 ....

10 ....

11 ....

12 ....

1 ....

2 ....

3 ....

4 ....

5 ....

6 ....

7 ....

8 ....

WHAT HAVE YOU DONE TOWARDS ACHIEVING YOUR WHEEL OF LIFE GOALS?

Family

Business

Career

Fun

THIS WEEK'S BIG TARGET:

Thursday

1 thing I must do:

3 actions/activities:

- ....
- ....
- ....

8
9
10
11
12
1
2
3
4
5
6
7
8

Friday

1 thing I must do:

3 actions/activities:

- ....
- ....
- ....

8
9
10
11
12
1
2
3
4
5
6
7
8

Saturday

1 thing I must do:

3 actions/activities:

- ....
- ....
- ....

8
9
10
11
12
1
2
3
4
5
6
7
8

Sunday

1 thing I must do:

3 actions/activities:

- ....
- ....
- ....

8
9
10
11
12
1
2
3
4
5
6
7
8

Social

Health

Finance

Wellbeing/Spiritual

Who Had The Most Impact?

The Best Conversation?

What Inspired You?

How Were You Brave?

What Made You Happy?

One Word Summary

What Did You Avoid?

Best Moment?

217

Weekly Review, week 13

On a scale of 1–10, how has this week been?

What would +1 look like?

What has worked well this week?

This week would have been even better if…

As we approach the end of the quarter, what have you failed to do?

What do you need to check?

Who do you still need to contact?

Q3 Quarterly Review

What do you feel were your most significant accomplishments?

Professional/Business:

Personal/Family:

What do you feel were your most significant disappointments?

Professional/Business:

Personal/Family:

Q3 Quarterly Business Review

AREA/INITIATIVE	SCORE OUT OF 10	WHY
FINANCIAL:		
MARKETING:		
OPERATIONS:		
PEOPLE & CULTURE:		
OTHER:		

Q3 Quarterly Personal Review

AREA/INITIATIVE	SCORE OUT OF 10	WHY
FAMILY		
BUSINESS		
CAREER		
FUN		
SOCIAL		
HEALTH		
FINANCE		
WELLBEING/SPIRITUAL		

NOTES

NOTES

NOTES

Q4 Quarterly Business Plan

Instructions: This quarterly plan should be created by looking at the annual plan on page 35 and applying the relevant data to this quarter.

AREA/INITIATIVE	BUDGET	WHO	WHEN
FINANCIAL:			
MARKETING:			
OPERATIONS:			
PEOPLE:			
OTHER:			

Q4 Quarterly Personal Plan

Instructions: This quarterly plan should be created by looking at the annual personal plan on page 42 and applying the relevant data to this quarter.

AREA/INITIATIVE	OUTCOME	WHEN
FAMILY		
BUSINESS		
CAREER		
FUN		
SOCIAL		
HEALTH		
FINANCE		
WELLBEING/SPIRITUAL		

Weekly Preview, week 1

Weekly Check-In Preview

Must do/urgent:

Must do/important:

Waiting/pending:

Delegate:

Carry forward:

1-CHECK: What's the *one* thing I *must* do this week (that will make other things easier or unnecessary):

1

3-CHECK: What are three projects/activities/actions that *must* be completed:

1

2

3

Weekly Planning, week 1

THIS WEEK'S BIG GOAL:

Monday

1 thing I must do:

3 actions/activities:

- ....
- ....
- ....

8

9

10

11

12

1

2

3

4

5

6

7

8

Tuesday

1 thing I must do:

3 actions/activities:

- ....
- ....
- ....

8

9

10

11

12

1

2

3

4

5

6

7

8

Wednesday

1 thing I must do:

3 actions/activities:

- ....
- ....
- ....

8

9

10

11

12

1

2

3

4

5

6

7

8

WHAT HAVE YOU DONE TOWARDS ACHIEVING YOUR WHEEL OF LIFE GOALS?

Family

Business

Career

Fun

THIS WEEK'S BIG TARGET:

Thursday

1 thing I must do:

3 actions/activities:

- ....
- ....
- ....

8

9

10

11

12

1

2

3

4

5

6

7

8

Friday

1 thing I must do:

3 actions/activities:

- ....
- ....
- ....

8

9

10

11

12

1

2

3

4

5

6

7

8

Saturday

1 thing I must do:

3 actions/activities:

- ....
- ....
- ....

8

9

10

11

12

1

2

3

4

5

6

7

8

Sunday

1 thing I must do:

3 actions/activities:

- ....
- ....
- ....

8

9

10

11

12

1

2

3

4

5

6

7

8

Social

Health

Finance

Wellbeing/Spiritual

Who Had The Most Impact?

The Best Conversation?

What Inspired You?

How Were You Brave?

What Made You Happy?

One Word Summary

What Did You Avoid?

Best Moment?

Weekly Review, week 1

On a scale of 1–10, how has this week been? ....

What would +1 look like? ....

What has worked well this week? ....

....

....

....

....

....

This week would have been even better if... ....

What I gave to others is: ....

What I received from others is: ....

What I appreciated: ....

Weekly Preview, week 2

Weekly Check-In Preview

Must do/urgent:

Must do/important:

Waiting/pending:

Delegate:

Carry forward:

1-CHECK: What's the *one* thing I *must* do this week (that will make other things easier or unnecessary):

1

3-CHECK: What are three projects/activities/actions that *must* be completed:

1

2

3

Weekly Planning, week 2

Monday

1 thing I must do:

3 actions/activities:

-
-
-

8

9

10

11

12

1

2

3

4

5

6

7

8

Tuesday

1 thing I must do:

3 actions/activities:

-
-
-

8

9

10

11

12

1

2

3

4

5

6

7

8

Wednesday

1 thing I must do:

3 actions/activities:

-
-
-

8

9

10

11

12

1

2

3

4

5

6

7

8

WHAT HAVE YOU DONE TOWARDS ACHIEVING YOUR WHEEL OF LIFE GOALS?

Family

Business

Career

Fun

THIS WEEK'S BIG TARGET:

Thursday

1 thing I must do:

3 actions/activities:

- ....
- ....
- ....

8
9
10
11
12
1
2
3
4
5
6
7
8

Friday

1 thing I must do:

3 actions/activities:

- ....
- ....
- ....

8
9
10
11
12
1
2
3
4
5
6
7
8

Saturday

1 thing I must do:

3 actions/activities:

- ....
- ....
- ....

8
9
10
11
12
1
2
3
4
5
6
7
8

Sunday

1 thing I must do:

3 actions/activities:

- ....
- ....
- ....

8
9
10
11
12
1
2
3
4
5
6
7
8

Social

Health

Finance

Wellbeing/Spiritual

Who Had The Most Impact?

The Best Conversation?

What Inspired You?

How Were You Brave?

What Made You Happy?

One Word Summary

What Did You Avoid?

Best Moment?

Weekly Review, week 2

On a scale of 1–10, how has this week been?

What would +1 look like?

What has worked well this week?

This week would have been even better if...

I love what I do because:

What do I need to start doing?

The elephant in the room that needs addressing is:

Weekly Preview, week 3

Weekly Check-In Preview

Must do/urgent:

Must do/important:

Waiting/pending:

Delegate:

Carry forward:

1-CHECK: What's the *one* thing I *must* do this week (that will make other things easier or unnecessary):

1

3-CHECK: What are three projects/activities/actions that *must* be completed:

1

2

3

Weekly Planning, week 3

THIS WEEK'S BIG GOAL:

Monday

1 thing I must do:

3 actions/activities:

- ....
- ....
- ....

8

9

10

11

12

1

2

3

4

5

6

7

8

Tuesday

1 thing I must do:

3 actions/activities:

- ....
- ....
- ....

8

9

10

11

12

1

2

3

4

5

6

7

8

Wednesday

1 thing I must do:

3 actions/activities:

- ....
- ....
- ....

8

9

10

11

12

1

2

3

4

5

6

7

8

WHAT HAVE YOU DONE TOWARDS ACHIEVING YOUR WHEEL OF LIFE GOALS?

Family

Business

Career

Fun

THIS WEEK'S BIG TARGET:

Thursday

1 thing I must do:

3 actions/activities:

- ....
- ....
- ....

8
9
10
11
12
1
2
3
4
5
6
7
8

Friday

1 thing I must do:

3 actions/activities:

- ....
- ....
- ....

8
9
10
11
12
1
2
3
4
5
6
7
8

Saturday

1 thing I must do:

3 actions/activities:

- ....
- ....
- ....

8
9
10
11
12
1
2
3
4
5
6
7
8

Sunday

1 thing I must do:

3 actions/activities:

- ....
- ....
- ....

8
9
10
11
12
1
2
3
4
5
6
7
8

Social

Health

Finance

Wellbeing/Spiritual

Who Had The Most Impact?

The Best Conversation?

What Inspired You?

How Were You Brave?

What Made You Happy?

One Word Summary

What Did You Avoid?

Best Moment?

Weekly Review, week 3

On a scale of 1–10, how has this week been?

What would +1 look like?

What has worked well this week?

This week would have been even better if...

Where's the focus?

The most important upcoming meeting is:

What do I need to change and why?

Weekly Preview, week 4

Weekly Check-In Preview

Must do/urgent:

Must do/important:

Waiting/pending:

Delegate:

Carry forward:

1-CHECK: What's the *one* thing I *must* do this week (that will make other things easier or unnecessary):

1

3-CHECK: What are three projects/activities/actions that *must* be completed:

1

2

3

Weekly Planning, week 4

THIS WEEK'S BIG GOAL:

Monday

1 thing I must do:

3 actions/activities:

- ....
- ....
- ....

8

9

10

11

12

1

2

3

4

5

6

7

8

Tuesday

1 thing I must do:

3 actions/activities:

- ....
- ....
- ....

8

9

10

11

12

1

2

3

4

5

6

7

8

Wednesday

1 thing I must do:

3 actions/activities:

- ....
- ....
- ....

8

9

10

11

12

1

2

3

4

5

6

7

8

WHAT HAVE YOU DONE TOWARDS ACHIEVING YOUR WHEEL OF LIFE GOALS?

Family

Business

Career

Fun

THIS WEEK'S BIG TARGET:

Thursday	Friday	Saturday	Sunday
1 thing I must do:	**1 thing I must do:**	**1 thing I must do:**	**1 thing I must do:**
3 actions/activities:	3 actions/activities:	3 actions/activities:	3 actions/activities:

Thursday

1 thing I must do:

3 actions/activities:

-
-
-

8
9
10
11
12
1
2
3
4
5
6
7
8

Friday

1 thing I must do:

3 actions/activities:

-
-
-

8
9
10
11
12
1
2
3
4
5
6
7
8

Saturday

1 thing I must do:

3 actions/activities:

-
-
-

8
9
10
11
12
1
2
3
4
5
6
7
8

Sunday

1 thing I must do:

3 actions/activities:

-
-
-

8
9
10
11
12
1
2
3
4
5
6
7
8

Social

Health

Finance

Wellbeing/Spiritual

Who Had The Most Impact?

The Best Conversation?

What Inspired You?

How Were You Brave?

What Made You Happy?

One Word Summary

What Did You Avoid?

Best Moment?

Weekly Review, week 4

On a scale of 1–10, how has this week been?

What would +1 look like?

What has worked well this week?

This week would have been even better if...

Who do I need to thank and why?

One conversation I need to have:

What's holding me back?

Weekly Preview, week 5

Weekly Check-In Preview

Must do/urgent:

Must do/important:

Waiting/pending:

Delegate:

Carry forward:

1-CHECK: What's the *one* thing I *must* do this week (that will make other things easier or unnecessary):

1

3-CHECK: What are three projects/activities/actions that *must* be completed:

1

2

3

Weekly Planning, week 5

THIS WEEK'S BIG GOAL:

Monday

1 thing I must do:

3 actions/activities:

- ....
- ....
- ....

8
9
10
11
12
1
2
3
4
5
6
7
8

Tuesday

1 thing I must do:

3 actions/activities:

- ....
- ....
- ....

8
9
10
11
12
1
2
3
4
5
6
7
8

Wednesday

1 thing I must do:

3 actions/activities:

- ....
- ....
- ....

8
9
10
11
12
1
2
3
4
5
6
7
8

**WHAT HAVE YOU DONE TOWARDS ACHIEVING
YOUR WHEEL OF LIFE GOALS?**

Family

Business

Career

Fun

THIS WEEK'S BIG TARGET:

Thursday

1 thing I must do:

3 actions/activities:

- ....
- ....
- ....

8

9

10

11

12

1

2

3

4

5

6

7

8

Friday

1 thing I must do:

3 actions/activities:

- ....
- ....
- ....

8

9

10

11

12

1

2

3

4

5

6

7

8

Saturday

1 thing I must do:

3 actions/activities:

- ....
- ....
- ....

8

9

10

11

12

1

2

3

4

5

6

7

8

Sunday

1 thing I must do:

3 actions/activities:

- ....
- ....
- ....

8

9

10

11

12

1

2

3

4

5

6

7

8

Social

Health

Finance

Wellbeing/Spiritual

Who Had The Most Impact?

The Best Conversation?

What Inspired You?

How Were You Brave?

What Made You Happy?

One Word Summary

What Did You Avoid?

Best Moment?

Weekly Review, week 5

On a scale of 1–10, how has this week been?

What would +1 look like?

What has worked well this week?

This week would have been even better if...

What I gave to others is:

What I received from others is:

What I appreciated:

Weekly Preview, week 6

Weekly Check-In Preview

Must do/urgent:

Must do/important:

Waiting/pending:

Delegate:

Carry forward:

1-CHECK: What's the *one* thing I *must* do this week (that will make other things easier or unnecessary):

1

3-CHECK: What are three projects/activities/actions that *must* be completed:

1

2

3

Weekly Planning, week 6

THIS WEEK'S BIG GOAL:

Monday

1 thing I must do:

3 actions/activities:

-
-
-

8

9

10

11

12

1

2

3

4

5

6

7

8

Tuesday

1 thing I must do:

3 actions/activities:

-
-
-

8

9

10

11

12

1

2

3

4

5

6

7

8

Wednesday

1 thing I must do:

3 actions/activities:

-
-
-

8

9

10

11

12

1

2

3

4

5

6

7

8

WHAT HAVE YOU DONE TOWARDS ACHIEVING YOUR WHEEL OF LIFE GOALS?

Family

Business

Career

Fun

THIS WEEK'S BIG TARGET:

Thursday

1 thing I must do:

3 actions/activities:

- ....
- ....
- ....

8
9
10
11
12
1
2
3
4
5
6
7
8

Friday

1 thing I must do:

3 actions/activities:

- ....
- ....
- ....

8
9
10
11
12
1
2
3
4
5
6
7
8

Saturday

1 thing I must do:

3 actions/activities:

- ....
- ....
- ....

8
9
10
11
12
1
2
3
4
5
6
7
8

Sunday

1 thing I must do:

3 actions/activities:

- ....
- ....
- ....

8
9
10
11
12
1
2
3
4
5
6
7
8

Social

Health

Finance

Wellbeing/Spiritual

Who Had The Most Impact?

The Best Conversation?

What Inspired You?

How Were You Brave?

What Made You Happy?

One Word Summary

What Did You Avoid?

Best Moment?

Weekly Review, week 6

On a scale of 1–10, how has this week been?

What would +1 look like?

What has worked well this week?

This week would have been even better if…

I love what I do because:

What do I need to start doing?

The elephant in the room that needs addressing is:

Weekly Preview, week 7

Weekly Check-In Preview

Must do/urgent:

Must do/important:

Waiting/pending:

Delegate:

Carry forward:

1-CHECK: What's the *one* thing I *must* do this week (that will make other things easier or unnecessary):

1

3-CHECK: What are three projects/activities/actions that *must* be completed:

1

2

3

Weekly Planning, week 7

THIS WEEK'S BIG GOAL:

Monday

1 thing I must do:

3 actions/activities:

- ....
- ....
- ....

8
9
10
11
12
1
2
3
4
5
6
7
8

Tuesday

1 thing I must do:

3 actions/activities:

- ....
- ....
- ....

8
9
10
11
12
1
2
3
4
5
6
7
8

Wednesday

1 thing I must do:

3 actions/activities:

- ....
- ....
- ....

8
9
10
11
12
1
2
3
4
5
6
7
8

WHAT HAVE YOU DONE TOWARDS ACHIEVING YOUR WHEEL OF LIFE GOALS?

Family

Business

Career

Fun

THIS WEEK'S BIG TARGET:

Thursday	Friday	Saturday	Sunday

1 thing I must do:

3 actions/activities:

-
-
-

1 thing I must do:

3 actions/activities:

-
-
-

1 thing I must do:

3 actions/activities:

-
-
-

1 thing I must do:

3 actions/activities:

-
-
-

8

9

10

11

12

1

2

3

4

5

6

7

8

Social

Health

Finance

Wellbeing/Spiritual

Who Had The Most Impact?

The Best Conversation?

What Inspired You?

How Were You Brave?

What Made You Happy?

One Word Summary

What Did You Avoid?

Best Moment?

Weekly Review, week 7

On a scale of 1–10, how has this week been?

What would +1 look like?

What has worked well this week?

This week would have been even better if…

Where's the focus?

The most important upcoming meeting is:

What do I need to change and why?

Weekly Preview, week 8

Weekly Check-In Preview

Must do/urgent:

Must do/important:

Waiting/pending:

Delegate:

Carry forward:

1-CHECK: What's the *one* thing I *must* do this week (that will make other things easier or unnecessary):

1

3-CHECK: What are three projects/activities/actions that *must* be completed:

1

2

3

Weekly Planning, week 8

Monday

1 thing I must do:

3 actions/activities:

- ....
- ....
- ....

8

9

10

11

12

1

2

3

4

5

6

7

8

Tuesday

1 thing I must do:

3 actions/activities:

- ....
- ....
- ....

8

9

10

11

12

1

2

3

4

5

6

7

8

Wednesday

1 thing I must do:

3 actions/activities:

- ....
- ....
- ....

8

9

10

11

12

1

2

3

4

5

6

7

8

WHAT HAVE YOU DONE TOWARDS ACHIEVING YOUR WHEEL OF LIFE GOALS?

Family

Business

Career

Fun

THIS WEEK'S BIG TARGET:

Thursday

1 thing I must do:

3 actions/activities:

-
-
-

8

9

10

11

12

1

2

3

4

5

6

7

8

Friday

1 thing I must do:

3 actions/activities:

-
-
-

8

9

10

11

12

1

2

3

4

5

6

7

8

Saturday

1 thing I must do:

3 actions/activities:

-
-
-

8

9

10

11

12

1

2

3

4

5

6

7

8

Sunday

1 thing I must do:

3 actions/activities:

-
-
-

8

9

10

11

12

1

2

3

4

5

6

7

8

Social

Health

Finance

Wellbeing/Spiritual

Who Had The Most Impact?

The Best Conversation?

What Inspired You?

How Were You Brave?

What Made You Happy?

One Word Summary

What Did You Avoid?

Best Moment?

Weekly Review, week 8

On a scale of 1–10, how has this week been?

What would +1 look like?

What has worked well this week?

This week would have been even better if…

Who do I need to thank and why?

One conversation I need to have:

What's holding me back?

Weekly Preview, week 9

Weekly Check-In Preview

Must do/urgent:

Must do/important:

Waiting/pending:

Delegate:

Carry forward:

1-CHECK: What's the *one* thing I *must* do this week (that will make other things easier or unnecessary):

1

3-CHECK: What are three projects/activities/actions that *must* be completed:

1

2

3

Weekly Planning, week 9

THIS WEEK'S BIG GOAL:

Monday

1 thing I must do:

3 actions/activities:

- ....
- ....
- ....

8 ....
9 ....
10 ....
11 ....
12 ....
1 ....
2 ....
3 ....
4 ....
5 ....
6 ....
7 ....
8 ....

Tuesday

1 thing I must do:

3 actions/activities:

- ....
- ....
- ....

8 ....
9 ....
10 ....
11 ....
12 ....
1 ....
2 ....
3 ....
4 ....
5 ....
6 ....
7 ....
8 ....

Wednesday

1 thing I must do:

3 actions/activities:

- ....
- ....
- ....

8 ....
9 ....
10 ....
11 ....
12 ....
1 ....
2 ....
3 ....
4 ....
5 ....
6 ....
7 ....
8 ....

WHAT HAVE YOU DONE TOWARDS ACHIEVING YOUR WHEEL OF LIFE GOALS?

Family

Business

Career

Fun

THIS WEEK'S BIG TARGET:

Thursday

1 thing I must do:

3 actions/activities:

- _____
- _____
- _____

8
9
10
11
12
1
2
3
4
5
6
7
8

Friday

1 thing I must do:

3 actions/activities:

- _____
- _____
- _____

8
9
10
11
12
1
2
3
4
5
6
7
8

Saturday

1 thing I must do:

3 actions/activities:

- _____
- _____
- _____

8
9
10
11
12
1
2
3
4
5
6
7
8

Sunday

1 thing I must do:

3 actions/activities:

- _____
- _____
- _____

8
9
10
11
12
1
2
3
4
5
6
7
8

Social

Health

Finance

Wellbeing/Spiritual

Who Had The Most Impact?

The Best Conversation?

What Inspired You?

How Were You Brave?

What Made You Happy?

One Word Summary

What Did You Avoid?

Best Moment?

Weekly Review, week 9

On a scale of 1–10, how has this week been? ....

What would +1 look like? ....

What has worked well this week? ....

....

....

....

This week would have been even better if… ....

What I gave to others is: ....

What I received from others is: ....

What I appreciated: ....

Weekly Preview, week 10

Weekly Check-In Preview

Must do/urgent:

Must do/important:

Waiting/pending:

Delegate:

Carry forward:

1-CHECK: What's the *one* thing I *must* do this week (that will make other things easier or unnecessary):

1

3-CHECK: What are three projects/activities/actions that *must* be completed:

1

2

3

Weekly Planning, week 10

THIS WEEK'S BIG GOAL:

Monday

1 thing I must do:

3 actions/activities:

- ....
- ....
- ....

8

9

10

11

12

1

2

3

4

5

6

7

8

Tuesday

1 thing I must do:

3 actions/activities:

- ....
- ....
- ....

8

9

10

11

12

1

2

3

4

5

6

7

8

Wednesday

1 thing I must do:

3 actions/activities:

- ....
- ....
- ....

8

9

10

11

12

1

2

3

4

5

6

7

8

WHAT HAVE YOU DONE TOWARDS ACHIEVING YOUR WHEEL OF LIFE GOALS?

Family

Business

Career

Fun

THIS WEEK'S BIG TARGET:

Thursday

1 thing I must do:

3 actions/activities:

- ·........................
- ·........................
- ·........................

8 ....
9 ....
10 ....
11 ....
12 ....
1 ....
2 ....
3 ....
4 ....
5 ....
6 ....
7 ....
8 ....

Friday

1 thing I must do:

3 actions/activities:

- ·........................
- ·........................
- ·........................

8 ....
9 ....
10 ....
11 ....
12 ....
1 ....
2 ....
3 ....
4 ....
5 ....
6 ....
7 ....
8 ....

Saturday

1 thing I must do:

3 actions/activities:

- ·........................
- ·........................
- ·........................

8 ....
9 ....
10 ....
11 ....
12 ....
1 ....
2 ....
3 ....
4 ....
5 ....
6 ....
7 ....
8 ....

Sunday

1 thing I must do:

3 actions/activities:

- ·........................
- ·........................
- ·........................

8 ....
9 ....
10 ....
11 ....
12 ....
1 ....
2 ....
3 ....
4 ....
5 ....
6 ....
7 ....
8 ....

Social

Health

Finance

Wellbeing/Spiritual

Who Had The Most Impact?

The Best Conversation?

What Inspired You?

How Were You Brave?

What Made You Happy?

One Word Summary

What Did You Avoid?

Best Moment?

Weekly Review, week 10

On a scale of 1–10, how has this week been?

What would +1 look like?

What has worked well this week?

This week would have been even better if...

I love what I do because:

What do I need to start doing?

The elephant in the room that needs addressing is:

Weekly Preview, week 11

Weekly Check-In Preview

Must do/urgent:

Must do/important:

Waiting/pending:

Delegate:

Carry forward:

1-CHECK: What's the *one* thing I *must* do this week (that will make other things easier or unnecessary):

1

3-CHECK: What are three projects/activities/actions that *must* be completed:

1

2

3

Weekly Planning, week 11

THIS WEEK'S BIG GOAL:

Monday

1 thing I must do:

3 actions/activities:

-
-
-

8

9

10

11

12

1

2

3

4

5

6

7

8

Tuesday

1 thing I must do:

3 actions/activities:

-
-
-

8

9

10

11

12

1

2

3

4

5

6

7

8

Wednesday

1 thing I must do:

3 actions/activities:

-
-
-

8

9

10

11

12

1

2

3

4

5

6

7

8

WHAT HAVE YOU DONE TOWARDS ACHIEVING YOUR WHEEL OF LIFE GOALS?

Family

Business

Career

Fun

THIS WEEK'S BIG TARGET:

Thursday

1 thing I must do:

3 actions/activities:

-
-
-

8

9

10

11

12

1

2

3

4

5

6

7

8

Friday

1 thing I must do:

3 actions/activities:

-
-
-

8

9

10

11

12

1

2

3

4

5

6

7

8

Saturday

1 thing I must do:

3 actions/activities:

-
-
-

8

9

10

11

12

1

2

3

4

5

6

7

8

Sunday

1 thing I must do:

3 actions/activities:

-
-
-

8

9

10

11

12

1

2

3

4

5

6

7

8

Social

Health

Finance

Wellbeing/Spiritual

Who Had The Most Impact?

The Best Conversation?

What Inspired You?

How Were You Brave?

What Made You Happy?

One Word Summary

What Did You Avoid?

Best Moment?

Weekly Review, week 11

On a scale of 1–10, how has this week been? ....

What would +1 look like? ....

What has worked well this week? ....

....

....

....

This week would have been even better if... ....

Where's the focus? ....

The most important upcoming meeting is: ....

What do I need to change and why? ....

Weekly Preview, week 12

Weekly Check-In Preview

Must do/urgent:

Must do/important:

Waiting/pending:

Delegate:

Carry forward:

1-CHECK: What's the *one* thing I *must* do this week (that will make other things easier or unnecessary):

1

3-CHECK: What are three projects/activities/actions that *must* be completed:

1

2

3

Weekly Planning, week 12

THIS WEEK'S BIG GOAL:

Monday

1 thing I must do:

3 actions/activities:

-
-
-

8

9

10

11

12

1

2

3

4

5

6

7

8

Tuesday

1 thing I must do:

3 actions/activities:

-
-
-

8

9

10

11

12

1

2

3

4

5

6

7

8

Wednesday

1 thing I must do:

3 actions/activities:

-
-
-

8

9

10

11

12

1

2

3

4

5

6

7

8

WHAT HAVE YOU DONE TOWARDS ACHIEVING YOUR WHEEL OF LIFE GOALS?

Family

Business

Career

Fun

Thursday	Friday	Saturday	Sunday

1 thing I must do: (Thursday)

3 actions/activities:

-
-
-

8
9
10
11
12
1
2
3
4
5
6
7
8

1 thing I must do: (Friday)

3 actions/activities:

-
-
-

8
9
10
11
12
1
2
3
4
5
6
7
8

1 thing I must do: (Saturday)

3 actions/activities:

-
-
-

8
9
10
11
12
1
2
3
4
5
6
7
8

1 thing I must do: (Sunday)

3 actions/activities:

-
-
-

8
9
10
11
12
1
2
3
4
5
6
7
8

Social

Health

Finance

Wellbeing/Spiritual

Who Had The Most Impact?

The Best Conversation?

What Inspired You?

How Were You Brave?

What Made You Happy?

One Word Summary

What Did You Avoid?

Best Moment?

Weekly Review, week 12

On a scale of 1–10, how has this week been? ....

What would +1 look like? ....

What has worked well this week? ....

....

....

....

....

This week would have been even better if... ....

Who do I need to thank and why? ....

One conversation I need to have: ....

What's holding me back? ....

Weekly Preview, week 13

Must do/urgent:

Must do/important:

Waiting/pending:

Delegate:

Carry forward:

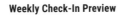

1-CHECK: What's the *one* thing I *must* do this week (that will make other things easier or unnecessary):

1

3-CHECK: What are three projects/activities/actions that *must* be completed:

1

2

3

Weekly Planning, week 13

THIS WEEK'S BIG GOAL:

Monday

1 thing I must do:

3 actions/activities:

- ....
- ....
- ....

8

9

10

11

12

1

2

3

4

5

6

7

8

Tuesday

1 thing I must do:

3 actions/activities:

- ....
- ....
- ....

8

9

10

11

12

1

2

3

4

5

6

7

8

Wednesday

1 thing I must do:

3 actions/activities:

- ....
- ....
- ....

8

9

10

11

12

1

2

3

4

5

6

7

8

WHAT HAVE YOU DONE TOWARDS ACHIEVING YOUR WHEEL OF LIFE GOALS?

Family

Business

Career

Fun

THIS WEEK'S BIG TARGET:

Thursday

1 thing I must do:

3 actions/activities:

- ....
- ....
- ....

8
9
10
11
12
1
2
3
4
5
6
7
8

Friday

1 thing I must do:

3 actions/activities:

- ....
- ....
- ....

8
9
10
11
12
1
2
3
4
5
6
7
8

Saturday

1 thing I must do:

3 actions/activities:

- ....
- ....
- ....

8
9
10
11
12
1
2
3
4
5
6
7
8

Sunday

1 thing I must do:

3 actions/activities:

- ....
- ....
- ....

8
9
10
11
12
1
2
3
4
5
6
7
8

Social

Health

Finance

Wellbeing/Spiritual

Who Had The Most Impact?

The Best Conversation?

What Inspired You?

How Were You Brave?

What Made You Happy?

One Word Summary

What Did You Avoid?

Best Moment?

Weekly Review, week 13

On a scale of 1–10, how has this week been?

What would +1 look like?

What has worked well this week?

This week would have been even better if…

As we approach the end of the quarter, what have you failed to do?

What do you need to check?

Who do you still need to contact?

Q4
Quarterly
Review

What do you feel were your most significant accomplishments?

Professional/Business:

Personal/Family:

What do you feel were your most significant disappointments?

Professional/Business:

Personal/Family:

Q4
Quarterly
Business
Review

AREA/INITIATIVE	SCORE OUT OF 10	WHY
FINANCIAL:		
MARKETING:		
OPERATIONS:		
PEOPLE & CULTURE:		
OTHER:		

Q4
Quarterly
Personal
Review

AREA/INITIATIVE	SCORE OUT OF 10	WHY
FAMILY		
BUSINESS		
CAREER		
FUN		
SOCIAL		
HEALTH		
FINANCE		
WELLBEING/SPIRITUAL		

NOTES

NOTES

Annual Review

What do you feel were your most significant accomplishments?
Professional/Business:

Personal/Family:

What do you feel were your most significant disappointments?
Professional/Business:

Personal/Family:

Annual Business Review

AREA/INITIATIVE	SCORE OUT OF 10	WHY
FINANCIAL:		
MARKETING:		
OPERATIONS:		
PEOPLE & CULTURE:		
OTHER:		

Annual Personal Review

AREA/INITIATIVE	SCORE OUT OF 10	WHY
FAMILY		
BUSINESS		
CAREER		
FUN		
SOCIAL		
HEALTH		
FINANCE		
WELLBEING/SPIRITUAL		

NOTES

NOTES

PART 3

ADDITIONAL MATERIAL AND RESOURCES

The following sections are additional materials to those in the opening Planning section of the Journal. There is also a plethora of other materials (case studies, examples, walk-throughs) on the website **www.checkinjournal.com/ thehub**.

It is one thing to run a "Strategy Away-day" to give you a grasp of *"Where are we now? Where are we going? How are we going to get there?"* However, making it happen is a very different kettle of fish.

One of the outputs from the Wallpaper exercise can be a more detailed plan: a simple but focused form of business plan.

Before you shriek in horror, we are not talking about a lengthy 250-page marathon.

We are talking about a clear explanation of the who, what, where, why, when and how (WWWWWH) of the various aspects of your business. Finance, marketing, operations and people and culture plans are the normal headings and the emphasis should be on targets and how you are going to achieve them.

The first four worksheets present the basic models or machines for finance, marketing, operations and people and culture. They help you to sum up and articulate the highlights of your model/system/process of working. Then, the "dashboard for the journey"...

Finance machine

Your one-year plan (WWWWWH):

BASIC NUMBERS:

Turnover:

Net profit:

Cash-flow:

Most profitable customers:

Least profitable customers:

Describe your Finance model:

Cost of customer acquisition:

Average lifetime value of a customer:

Average transaction value:

Products/services:

Marketing machine

Your one-year plan (WWWWWWH):

Your target market is:

Three things that make you unique are:

Describe your Marketing machine – the client acquisition journey:

Operations machine

Your one-year plan (WWWWWH):

Three things that make you unique are:

Describe your Operations machine:

People and Culture machine

Your one-year plan (WWWWWH):

Three things that make you unique are:

Describe your People and Culture machine:

A dashboard for the journey

On a monthly basis your senior management team (or board) needs to meet to track progress against the Wallpaper.

We suggest a simple dashboard to tell you the basics.

Referring back to the FiMO-PC score exercise, we would opt for a maximum of four measures in each of four boxes as follows:

- Finance
- Marketing
- Operations
- People and culture and growth.

This dashboard is like the dials in an airplane cockpit measuring the critical and vital things:

- How high?
- How much fuel?
- How fast are we going?
- How far to go?

In the case of your business, you measure the things (both quantitative and qualitative) that will be indicators of how you are doing.

This exercise is worth its weight in gold. It will help you decide what is and what is not important. It will help you to focus on the real results and not the vanity figures that can so easily distract us.

Action: Quick 'n' dirty

Select four measures for each of finance, marketing, operations, and people/culture/growth. You can use your KPI list from earlier. Make sure that measuring the criteria you choose will inform you of your performance.

In real time, this exercise should come *after* agreeing your *purpose*, *vision*, *mission*, *strategy* and *milestones*.

To see more about how to set up effective and practical dashboards (AKA scorecards), go to the website **www.checkjournal.com/thehub**.

GLOSSARY

Accountability

The acknowledgement and the assumption of responsibility for actions, decisions and results.

Balanced Business Scorecard

Measuring the key indicators for your business, typically 16 in total. Often referred to as the Scorecard or Dashboard.

Big Hairy Audacious Goal (BHAG)

A long-term goal that changes the very nature of a business' existence. See *Built to Last* (Collins & Poras).

Cascade

The process of defining your plan: Purpose, Vision, Mission, Strategy, Milestones, Key Performance Indicators.

Check-in

Reflect on last week's performance and next week's challenges.

Core Success Factor (CSF)

Step on the way or milestone.

Culture

How we do things around here.

Dashboard

Scorecard.

FiMO

Finance, Marketing and Operations – the top of the FiMO-PC exercise.

Key Performance Indicator (KPI)

A business metric used to evaluate factors that are crucial to the success of an organisation.

Mastermind Group

The coordination of knowledge and effort of two or more people who work toward a definite purpose, in the spirit of harmony. (Napoleon Hill.)

Milestone

Step on the way or a core success factor (CSF).

Mission

What numbers do you want to hit?

P&C

People and Culture.

PI

Performance indicator.

State of the Nation (SOTN)

A monthly report for the boardroom covering key issues only.

Strategy

Planning while being aware of the outside environment.

Vision

What do you want to be known for?

Wallpaper Exercise

Mapping out the plan for the next three years on wallpaper – defining the journey.

WWWWWH

Who, what, where, when, why and how.

One-point CHECK

What's the one thing, that if we did it, then other things would become less necessary or unnecessary?

Three-point CHECKlist

What are the three things that are a must?

BIBLIOGRAPHY AND FURTHER READING

Armstrong, Michael, *How to Be an Even More Effective Manager*, Kogan Page, 1994

Carroll, Lewis, *Alice's Adventures in Wonderland*, Collins, 2010

Collins JC & Poras JI, *Built To Last*, Random House, 2005

Collins, Sam, *Work The System*, Greenleaf, 2014

Collis DJ & Rukstad MG, *Can You Say What Your Strategy Is?*, HBR, April 2008

Covey, Stephen, *Seven Habits of Highly Effective People*, Simon & Schuster, 1999

Craven, Robert, *Customer Is King*, Virgin Books, 2005

Craven, Robert, *Kick-Start Your Business*, Virgin Books, 2005

Craven, Robert, *Bright Marketing*, Crimson Books, 2007

Craven, Robert, *Grow Your Service Firm*, Crimson Books, 2012

Ditzler, Jenny, *Your Best Year Yet*, Harper, 1996

Duhigg, Charles, *The Power of Habit – Why We Do What We Do*, Random House, 2102

Ferriss, Tim, *The 4-Hour Workweek*, Crown, 2007

Gawande, Atul, *The Checklist Manifesto*, Profile, 2011

Goldsmith, Marshall, *What Got You Here Won't Get You There*, Profile, 2008

Hill, Napoleon, *Think and Grow Rich*, Mindpower Press, 2015

Hsieh, Tony, *Delivering Happiness: A Path to Profits, Passion, and Purpose*, Plus, 2010

Johnson, Alexandra, *Leaving a Trace: On Keeping a Journal*, Back Bay Books, 2002

Kaplan RS & Norton DP, *Strategy Maps: Converting Intangible Assets into Tangible Outcomes*, Harvard Press, 2003

Keller G & Papasan J, *The One Thing*, John Murray, 2013

Lencioni, Patrick, *The Five Dysfunctions of the Team*, Jossey-Bass, 2002

Sharma, Robin, *Leadership Wisdom from the Monk Who Sold His Ferrari*, Harper 2010

Sinek, Simon, *Leaders Eat Last: Why Some Teams Pull Together and Others Don't*, Penguin, 2014

Tracy, Brian, *Eat That Frog*, Hodder, 2013

Is this the end?

In no way are we at the end.

Next year

The Check-in Journal, for many, becomes a way of life. So you can order next year's in advance, use the code "NEXT" to receive your discount. We also offer discounts for orders of five copies or more.

A bespoke Journal experience for your organisation?

If you are interested in having bespoke copies specific to your organisation, then let's talk.

Keynotes, conferences and seminars and workshops

Both Robert and Adam are regular speakers at conferences and workshops. Clients include Google, Barclays, Vistage, and ACE.

Consultancy

Both Robert and Adam work with clients on a consultancy basis.

How else can we stay in contact?

Adam and Robert run workshops and seminars as well as delivering keynotes to help you run an even more effective organisation. Call us on (+44)1225 851044.

About the companion website

While this Journal is clearly a stand-alone resource, there are also some essential resources that will help you to get the maximum benefit:

- Access to book-owners-only resources

  A series of interviews, case studies and how-tos covering every exercise in the Journal and much, much more from Robert and Adam: www.checkinjournal.com.

- Join our community on social media
  - Twitter www.twitter.com/checkinjournal
  - Facebook www.facebook.com/CheckinStrategyJournal
  - Instagram www.instagram.com/checkinstrategyjournal
  - LinkedIn www.linkedin.com/groups/8556651
  - YouTube http://bit.ly/2ea3FHf.

ABOUT THE AUTHORS

Robert Craven works with ambitious owner-directors of fast-growing businesses who feel that they could be doing even better.

Robert set up the first of several businesses (restaurant, cafe, training company, sound studio) in his final year at university. He then spent five years running training and consultancy programmes for entrepreneurs at *Warwick Business School*. Running his own consultancy – The Directors' Centre – since 1998, he is now one of the UK's best-known speakers on growing your business.

Alongside numerous speaking engagements, Robert also does consulting work for, and is chairman or personal mentor to, a number of growing UK businesses.

He lives near Bath with his wife and two Jack Russells; his three fabulous children have escaped to live their own lives!

Contact Details

E: rc@checkinjournal.com

W: www.robert-craven.com

Twitter: @robert_craven

LinkedIn: www.linkedin.com/in/robertcraven

T: +44 (0)1225 851044

Books by Robert Craven

Grow Your Digital Agency, Directors' Centre, 2015

Crunch Questions, Directors' Centre, 2013

Grow Your Service Firm, Crimson, 2012

Bright Marketing For Small Businesses, Crimson, 2011

Beating The Credit Crunch, Directors' Centre, 2008

Bright Marketing: Why Should People..., Crimson, 2007

The Start-Up Essays, Directors' Centre, 2004

Customer Is King, Virgin, 2002/14

Kick-Start Your Business, Virgin, 2001/5

Robert also co-authored:

Great British Entrepreneur's Handbook 2015, Harriman House, 2015

Business Gurus, Crimson, 2012

Adam Harris is a serial (and often successful) business leader, owner and innovator, with a keen understanding of the value of strategic connections. He has an equally ardent aversion to clutter, noise, fluff and drudgery that gets in the way of our success.

As the Introducer, he seeks to acquaint us not only with the power of networks, but with enhanced results and greater opportunity.

He can help leaders and executive teams determine who they need to know, and who and what they need to know, to produce sustainable business and personal results.

Adam established his business consultancy, Fresh Mindset by The Introducer, in 2010, and has worked with CEOs and senior managers providing training, coaching and high-level peer group activities to convert opportunities into successes, drive profit, facilitate change, define company direction and leverage the network.

Adam lives in Derbyshire with his wife and two young daughters, who keep him well and truly on his toes.

Contact Details

E: adam@checkinjournal.com

W: www.fresh-mindset.com

Twitter: @freshmindset1

LinkedIn: www.linkedin.com/in/aharris1

T: +44 (0)1225 851044

The Directors' Centre

The Directors' Centre works with ambitious directors and owners of businesses who have concerns about the way their business is growing – they are growing too quickly or not quickly enough!

Clients work with us because we are challenging, honest and goading. Because we help them run the business they really want to run.

The team knows how to grow a business because they have all been there and done it... which means that you get straightforward, no-nonsense solutions to your problems.

Contact details

E: office@directorscentre.com

W: **www.directorscentre.com**

T: +44 (0)1225 851044

NOTES

NOTES